MW00761090

Three Strikes

Graduating from the University of Adversity

To My friend BARBARA with much love. Diedra

by
Diedra Cole

Diedra Cole
10/1/2005

Published by

The Empty Canoe, LLC

Oak Harbor

www.emptycanoe.com

ISBN: 0-9749933-5-2

Acknowledgements

I would like to thank and acknowledge the following people for all their help in the growth of the University of Adversity:

Minister David Hollowell

Dr Felicia Jamison

James Vance

Rev. Dr. Cleo LaRue

Thank you for your support. Your efforts do not go unnoticed…

Introduction

Where are we as individuals, as a nation, and as a race? This is a question the nation asks as we pass the 50th anniversary of integrating our schools. The integration era ushered in scenarios of black children sitting beside white children, regardless of whether either wanted it or not. It was a different time then, no question. People were vocal about their beliefs in 1954; loud and strong were the dissenting white voices, while the black voices cried out their passionate pleas. One wanted status quo, and the other wanted status. It was a time when people were not afraid of their cause because they believed in it no matter which side they lined up on. Riots filled the streets, men were hung by ropes, children were beaten, and teens were killed. Local police sanctioned much of this conduct in parts of the country. Washington was asking, no... telling states how they should act but many of these states, especially in the Deep South with their Civil War heritage, refused to obey the federal government.

It was a time when many Americans knew the disadvantages they were suffering. No matter how hard they tried to overcome those "faults," many sectors of society were told continuously that they were not allowed to compete. In tallying up the damage to themselves psychologically, socially, and economically, many in society began moving to a point where they had to make a decision about accepting their lot or fighting for their rights. The end result was a critical watershed moment when people throughout the country began demanding equal rights, no matter what the strikes against them.

In 1954, your strike was that you were black and it did not much matter your gender or your ability to get around. In that decade, this country had only moved forward by twenty years recognizing women had equal rights to men. The Suffrage movement was being transformed into feminism, the movement for Civil Rights for black Americans was growing, and we were still forty years from a real Americans with Disabilities Act. This is the history. Once upon a time it was questioned how much a person was worth based upon what they could offer the world. Mostly it was the corporate or educational world judging and sending people home if they were not middle class enough, conformist enough, white enough, or healthy enough. If you did not fit those types, the odds were you were not counted for much. We say it is now a different world. We say now it is a time and place where all Americans are treated equal. Again, how far have we come?

I will not try to answer that from a societal standpoint. Instead, I can answer from my own personal standpoint. As a black disabled woman, I have come far. Moreover, it was not society that got me here. Yes, there are programs I have benefited from that did not exist seventy, fifty, or even ten years ago. Those programs still put limitations on what is provided and limited their expectations of a disabled person. You can think we have come far and you would be correct in many ways.

It is not legal on the books anymore to do what once was legal. There are still strikes against us, though. No society can write in its laws the things I have found. No judge can enact any legislation to lift me as far as I have come. I have found my liberation outside of the law and outside of society. African Americans slaves, in the early and mid-1800's, found liberation in their soul. That liberation formed the gospel music found in church after church, from sanctuary to sanctuary, week after week. Amazing Grace. That is it, which is what my family gave me... the promise of Amazing Grace. Even with three strikes against me in the face of society, I was lifted above it all. Come with me. Hear my story and how I woke to find myself in a gigantic arena of learning, a University of Adversity.

I have what I consider three strikes, but you might have fewer or more depending on your situation. Life can throw a wrench at us and mess up our machinery in a wink. One day you are on top and the next you are off the radar. My life started out difficult and only through learning did I overcome. However, maybe you thought everything was fine until one day it was not. No matter whether you were born into a world of adversity or awoke to find yourself there, I have discovered the coursework that will get you a University of Adversity diploma.

Throughout this book, you will learn the following points.

· How to determine what your strikes are.

· How to take control of your life, even in the face of this adversity.

· How to pinpoint your strengths and enhance them.

· How to isolate your weaknesses and minimize them.

· How to create a world around you full of positive
   influences.

My first strike is that I am disabled. My second is that I am a woman. My third is that I am African-American. Add those three together and in most people's eyes I am at best a "special" case, and at worst a drain on society. The truth is that I am a productive citizen of this country with much to offer. If I had listened to those negative voices, I would never have come as far as I have. I am ready to share my story with you, and hope you can come to recognize your own strikes. Let us then isolate those strikes and help you discover how they can become strengths.

More than anything, we want you to recognize your strengths and have them raise you up to a place you never dreamed you would achieve. There is liberation in this country, but mostly there is liberation only within oneself. You need to surround yourself with people telling you that you can be what you want to be. You might want something that requires an education, but without the wherewithal to get that education. You might want to climb a ladder within your job you do not think is there for you to climb. You might strive for healing within your family you think can never be achieved. You might not even know what you want, but need a place that can help you define your goals. This is that book for you. Through my struggle for most all these issues, and my achievement of them, I will show you where I found the strength to move beyond my "place" society put me in. It is not involuntary or forced. We can be what we need to be through our own inner determination.

We will talk about this later in the book as well, but one other purpose this book serves is the idea of "paying forward" what is done for you. I am giving you hints and tips that helped changed my life. I ask when you finish that you tell others of this book. I am hoping that you hold onto this book for years, so you can keep coming back to it when you wake up one morning and wonder what there is to do in the face of a new adversity.

Life will throw adversity in our path almost daily. Of this, we can be certain. How will you handle these challenges? How will you approach these inevitable challenges? How will you change your life?

At the end of this book, we will have a moment where I again ask the tough questions. It is important you address these questions with respect, and a desire to change your life.

I promise the University of Adversity will change your life.

It changed mine.

.

Chapter One
Defense of the Strikes

The first thing to understand about adversity is the difference between what is beyond our control and what is within our control. One might be tempted to say this is the same as "what is real and what is not," but the truth is, even the stuff in our minds is real to us. However, we can control what is in our mind. What we cannot control are outside 'real' forces. As an example, when I was in college I had determined no matter what grades I earned, no matter how hard I worked, nobody would take me seriously once I graduated. In my town, an African American woman was not considered prime hiring material. Add to that a disability and I was out of the game. Whether this is a fact or not we will never know because I dropped out of college, convinced I was not employable. Do you see the difference? Real or not real is irrelevant if I thought it was real.

Our minds have a great deal of control over how we act day in and day out. Every morning we have the opportunity to decide this day is the day we make all the right choices, we think nothing but positive thoughts about ourselves, we will achieve one new goal, or set a new goal. Every single minute of every single day, we can make that choice.

However, we must be able to tell the difference between that which is real, and not real.

What do you think is real about your situation? As a student in the University of Adversity, you must open your mind to the idea that your current convictions might not be the same when we are done. Realize the way you feel right now is very real, but it is not necessarily the way God sees the situation. By graduation day, we are going to strive to see ourselves, and our world, through the eyes of God. Our world in both our eyes and God's eyes is not always beautiful. Friend, in God's eyes you are always beautiful.

I say graduation day, but I really just mean by the end of the book. We never really graduate from the University of Adversity. We will get more into this later, but for now suffice it to say these lessons are life lessons. We will not stop at the moment we have overcome our strikes. There will always be new days and new trials.

During slavery, my ancestors, and perhaps yours too, were told they were no better than animals. Animals were treated better than some of my people. How did they overcome this societal message that was supposed to be 'real' to them? In the beginning, they opened their minds and their souls to God. It was the truth that God saw them as human, that they were His children. The Bible says we have to come to God as children and with the unquestioning faith of children. They did. It is all they had. This faith kept them believing and struggling to disprove what society thought was real. In time, more and more learned to read, which opened up the world. Not only were their souls alive, but now their minds were alive. Mind, Body, and Soul. Reality was that society put them in a spot they could not fight out of until they believed slavery did not have to be their reality. Control what you can control- your own mind. Do not worry about what you cannot control because once your mind, body, and soul believe you can overcome adversity, then your reality will begin to change.

The situations we are in today are not nearly as bleak as the days when humans in our land were treated as animals. However, in our minds we sometimes believe, for real, that we are slaves to our situation. Decide right now that you are not a slave, and then answer these questions:

1. What else could you be doing other than what you are doing?

2. Who do you know that agrees you can change your situation? Talk to them.

3. List three other things you wish you could be doing this year. Now, list three for next year. Finally, list three for this month.

Here is a key to getting through what we will now call UA (University of Adversity): It is not what you know, but whom you know.

Making it through UA does not involve physical testing and other forms of class work. You will get through UA by opening your mind and getting closer to the Dean. It is not about knowledge, but about the ACT. The ACT is not an intelligence test. It does not test how well you have prepared. In the University of Adversity, there are two choices: Failure and Success. Two tests determine the outcome. One is the ACT and the other is the SAT. However, unlike normal University education where most require you take both tests, UA decides your outcome by which test you take. It is simple. The SAT is just that. You sat and did nothing. The ACT is Activating Change Together. You, me, neighbors, strangers… a group, everyone as a whole working and ACTing together. Not just creating change or making change but *activating* change.

It is your disposition, or how you ACT, which will determine your grade during your trial time through UA. God allows the tests to strengthen you, but your ACT is how you come through the test. Despite scoring low on my college entrance exams (SATs) I still persevered to get an Associate's degree in business management. There was a brief time when I just SAT because I felt there was no use in my attending school. I might as well sit now instead of working for more sitting later, I thought. Then I ACTed and earned, note I say *earned,* my degree. Disability in and of itself is a coarse course. How you ACT during the course determines the outcome. What is your choice?

You just made a short list of goals above. We will get more into goals later, but those will be starters. For every new goal you wrote, you probably have many reasons why you can never achieve those goals. But how many of those reasons are a result of simply sitting (SAT)? If you put a little ACT into action, how different could your life be? That is my point. I do not even want to figure the number of hours wasted on those with dreams who SAT instead of ACTed. If you want to overcome your adversity, you are going to have to get up and ACT.

What about the cost of UA? How much is tuition? As you might guess, it has already been paid. You are on a Dean's Scholarship, paid by the Dean himself. Back when I decided to drop out of the academic college, where the tests were paper and pencil, a good friend convinced me back into school. My guidance counselor, excited at my return, promised scholarships to keep me in the game. Therefore, I stayed under scholarship. However, my mind would not embrace this reality and when my English Composition II instructor recommended I take honors English, I turned it down. For one, I wanted to graduate and this class would have interrupted my graduation schedule. But more than that, I did not believe in myself. Another example of someone seeing potential in me that I could not see: I was a student at this academic University, but I was not taking classes in UA. I was a prisoner to this adversity I allowed to keep me down.

It was a clear-cut case of my reality (in my mind) being different than the reality of those around me. I could not get it in my own head how much they wanted from me. Not only how much they wanted, but also how much they knew I could do... how much more I could achieve. My head told me I would not make it through Honors English, so I did not even try.

Consider these questions:
- What lately has someone said to you that you should try and you said 'no'?
- Why did you say no? How could a 'yes' have changed your life?

ACT today and give a couple of your most recent "no's" a yes.

I was born in Orange, New Jersey. Diedra Cole was and is my name, and at birth I was given my first adversary-pneumonia.

Within days, I encountered my second. My nurse, who did not reveal this until much later, dropped me. My mother did not know, Nana did not know. I knew, but what could I do about it? When I was three months, my mother was informed that I had Cerebral Palsy. A sharp blow to the head can cause Cerebral Palsy. It is a condition (not a disease) of the brain, and while it is not curable, there are means to contain the negative progression or perhaps even reverse the muscle reaction to the brain damage. My condition was poor as an infant. Professionals advised my mother to place me in an institution, as I would be unable to function in society. My mother and grandmother stood firm in their belief that I would worsen in an environment where my condition was encouraged instead of challenged. Early on they put that part of me in UA, and we overcame.

My mother and grandmother believed a different reality from that which others told them: Even that of the doctors. They had choices to make about my future and took the road of overcoming adversity instead of giving into it.

CEREBRAL – *Adj.*

1. Of or relating to the brain or cerebrum.

2. Appealing to or requiring the use of intellect.

CEREBRAL –*Noun.*

A disorder usually caused by brain damage occurring at or before birth and marked by muscular impairment.

Just by definition CEREBRAL stigmatizes you.

The quality (aspect) of my life that I asked God to take away He did not grant. Instead, He used my affliction to reach people. I became a vessel, a container, carrying the qualities or characteristics of JESUS' life.

Nobody believed what the doctors told us about my future with a cerebral disability. I bet if I had said, "Someday I'm going to outline and put together a book about this," the doctors would have patted my shoulder and told my Nana not to let me dream too many big dreams.

You might ask how one can come to terms with the fact that their entire value as a person, seemingly devoid of all choices the majority of the population has, can look to the heavens and say, "Thank you God." It is easy, really, when you manipulate your mind to consider how to think of life not in terms of what is but of what we believe it is. You see? We have the choice to make our reality what we need it to be. We can let God have His way once we realize reality is in the eyes of God and not simply what is in our minds.

Live In Me Jesus – "Have Thine Own Way"

Have thine own way, Lord. Have thine own way. Not my will, but yours shall be done.

Until I was seven, I lived at home and attended classes and therapy at an Orthopedic School. When I turned seven, I went into Matheny School in Peapack, New Jersey, where I was put under strenuous therapy. Five years had passed, my condition improved in small doses, and my family unwavering pushed me to push my body against what we had been advised as an infant. There was nothing easy about this over achieving. I also had no choice. My momma and Nana gave me no other choice. I could not necessarily see within my own head this new reality, but they did. They saw my potential and would not let me give in to SAT. Meanwhile, while my body was learning to improve, my brain was working overtime academically.

In 1979, I broke from my peers at Matheny School and became the first physically disabled person to attend regular academic tracts in the South Orange/Maplewood school district. I graduated from Morris County College in 1997. I could not have done it without a loving, amazing family. I could not have done it without a loving God. Moreover, I could not have done it without courses in UA.

We have choices, every day, every hour, and literally every minute. You can choose to throw this book out the window. You can choose to shut the television off. You can choose to lose 100 pounds, dunk a basketball, write a novel, or even run for political office. Whatever is within your mind's eye, you can reach it. You must believe. You must believe you can overcome your strikes and overcome the voices around you telling you otherwise.

Ask and it will be given to you; seek and you will find; knock and the door will be opened to you. For everyone who asks receives, he who seeks finds; and to him who knocks, the door will be opened.

- Matthew 7:7-8

What is the UA curriculum?

The first understanding of UA curriculum is how life can change in a blink. Some are born with disabling conditions; others catch or develop symptoms over time. Any one at any age, any race, and any gender can be stricken with an affliction. Your world can be changed in a moment. Your comfort zone turned upside down. By default, we often slip into depression, feeling powerless and as if we do not have choices. However, once you are aware that life can change for anyone, anytime, you are ready for admittance. UA takes away that default reaction of depression and lifts you to a higher place, putting you in God's hands (or makes you aware you are always already there).

The idea is that you are simply prepared for whatever comes your way. Nothing can surprise you. You might feel shock, but you soon enough are ready to deal with new adversity because you realize this is what life does. Moreover, you never lose sight of your goals because this adversity is simply something that you have to overcome. It is not changing the course of your entire life. It cannot because you will not allow it.

My mother did not plan for her daughter named Diedra to struggle through life with a crippling condition. Life does not prepare you for surprises. Nobody gives you the Plan B if it does not go according to script. People who lost family in 9/11 had no idea that Tuesday morning would change everything. The baby born with Muscular Dystrophy puts the family in a position of taking care of a child they thought might one day be a star basketball player. Fire destroys homes and memories. Jobs are lost, families are broken, racism shatters dreams; the road of life is blocked with obstacles. It is never planned, but it happens all around.

If you accept this or if you have experienced this and you feel hopeless, take the Dean's scholarship and syllabus. No matter what you have experienced or where you are, you have dreams and goals. The University of Adversity will give you the course work you need to take back your life, and to raise up higher than you dreamed possible.

The First Semester

The semester begins when you feel at a loss. Your semester ends when life is good and you are comfortable. School starts again when the inevitable adversity returns. Past performance is not a guarantee of future results. Take each trial as they come. When the adversity is over, you get a spring (or summer or winter) break. Stay sharp for the next semester. Before I was ready to enter the school, I had to come to grips with my three strikes and realize they were, mentally, what kept me down. Would I have stayed in school if I were not disabled? I still had reservations that an African American woman was wanted in the job market. Would I have finished my degree if I were disabled but a black male? I cannot answer these questions because all I know is the combination of the three strikes were enough to keep me in my mental 'place.'

In between when you have overcome the latest adversity and when the next wrench is thrown your way, there are many around you having new unplanned problems. They might not be ready for this adversity. You need to be prepared to step in and help. You need to be prepared to instruct a little at the University.

Thank God for the University of Adversity.
Thank God for my Nana Cole.

You need a person in your life that acts as a role model. I tell you my story about my Nana, and how she kept me on the straight and narrow. How she kept me believing in myself. How she and my mother refused to believe I belonged in a home or kept separate from "normal" kids. To my Nana, I was normal. In my mind, I was not. However, somebody believes more in you than you believe in yourself. Find that person. Trust that person. Who is your influence? Who can you be a strong influence for?

· Name three people that believe in you.

· Name three people you in return believe in.

· Right now, is there anyone that you could give
  assistance to?

You have to believe in yourself before you can believe in someone else. The first steps of adversity are realizing you can pull through. Fruits of your knowledge should be shared with others needing your influence. Model your role model for another. In a world where kids have role models making millions of dollars, driving expensive cars, it is difficult to get a child or teen to think anything less is considered a success. When we think we have so far to go to get to those worldly rewards we again turn to desperate measures. You need to overcome your adversity to succeed on a level beyond wealth. Your level is contentment within. A role model who finds contentment within, who rises above where society wants to place them, has more worth to a child than the bank accounts of the rich and famous combined. God does not want us to store wealth on Earth, but to store our wealth in Heaven. Our heavenly bank is loaded from soul contentment.

How can a person be an influence without wealth and bling? It is easy, actually. Because what a kid (or friend) does not always see is someone that genuinely cares for them. My Nana was never rich, but she was rich in spirit and love. That kind of care to another kid or adult can be life changing both for you and for them.

The mission statement of the University of Adversity reads as follows:

"This institution's distinctive vocation is to equip students with the fortitude and disposition to profile and disseminate hope globally through personal adversities. This University is dedicated to serving the University community, and the worldwide networks of scholars."

Your course options include:

· Troubleshooting

· Communication Skills

· Perseverance

· Faith

· Disability (the coarse course)

Welcome to My World

Spiritual warfare and physical combat are both negative attacks on our lives, but while they work against us in the same way, they are very different. Spiritual warfare is that upon our soul and upon our hearts. Physical combat is rarely of a spiritual dimension. Physical is usually against others (mentally or by violence) or verbally.

Wisdom gained through physical combat is earthly wisdom. You learn how to navigate traffic (both auto and pedestrian). You learn where the disabled-friendly businesses are, where to shop, where to enjoy the outdoors. You learn where to fight your battles when others discriminate against you. There are times when you cannot control others and times when their actions can be stopped and even shamed when they are discriminating against others as well.

Wisdom through spiritual combat gets you closer to God. You will learn, because God is a God of battle (2 Chr. 32:8), you will overcome. You cannot lose a spiritual war with God on your side. It is not possible, and there is nothing more enriching. The earthly army would not accept me if I'd wanted to join because I'm not physically fit to fight in their war, but you don't have to be physically fit in God's Army or to have the gift of discernment. To discern is to perceive with the eyes or intellect. Discernment is a mental gift, the ability for the mind to know the difference between what is important and what is of this disposable world.

To have a gift of discernment you must be aware.

· Of the list earlier, concerning your biggest issues right now, which are physical and which are spiritual?
· How can God help with the spiritual issues?
· What can be done about the physical issues?

Learn to discern within your life the various issues and how they can affect your life.

What are the determining factors in choosing to enlist in the army rather than enrolling in school? Money. Opportunities. Goals (direction for your life). Travel. Convenience.

The University's motto: We are designed to strengthen your life in spite of your adversity. You can take coursework with you. We are mobile so if God wants you to move you can move and remain enrolled.

To overcome my three strikes I had to tackle the challenges of UA and allow God to lead me into my spiritual battles. Throughout history, those with the strike of a disability have not only been limited by choices, but society believed we should not have choices.

History of Disability

For whatever reasons, the history of this young country is littered with ideas of trash. In addition, in time, we have tried to sweep them away to the forgetful place, but there is no forgetting. We should not forget for fear of repeating mistakes. I cannot tell you why African Americans, women, and the disabled have been ignored or mistreated throughout history. In all cases, it was not until these issues were forced into the national spotlight that people took notice. Never has there been mistreatment or legislation protecting white males. There is a connection, but I think it goes deeper and perhaps broader than simple bigotry or elitism. I think it boils down to ignorance. What we do not know or what we do not understand both threatens and befuddles us. Therefore, let me give a quick history of the disability movement.

Going back as far as the Middle Ages there was discrimination against the disabled. To society, there was no value in a person unable to work at normal daily tasks. Without productivity, they felt there was no use for the disabled human. They were treated as objects of shame and considered outcasts. Much of the basis of this (and other social ills) was a result of religious misunderstanding or even misinterpretation. If a man or woman could not to support his or her family, in the eyes of God there was no use for them. Some went so far to suggest disability was a punishment from God. Deviance and disability were somehow connected. Over time, thankfully, small changes were made in societal thinking.

In the time period between the European Renaissance through to the establishment of an Independent nation forming the United States. The disabled were seen as human, but a special type of human (thus the term 'special needs'). The church and governments started providing services to these people that held up the cogs of productivity and freedom. After all, what is less free than physical shackles? Nobody argued that we were unable to perform all the normal functions of male and female, but enough believed we were charity cases that people began reaching out to help in the name of God. Still in ignorance of our abilities, the church feared that we, as the 'least of these,' if left ignored might cause Jesus himself to be ignored. After all, Jesus said what you do for the least of these you have done for me. We were given help in return for our bodies. We were studied to death for the betterment of those around us.

After the Civil War, around the mid to late 1850's, sweeping social reforms began. Private and government organizations began educational programs for uninformed citizens and the disabled. These programs provided an opportunity for those wanting knowledge to receive that knowledge. Corporations understood the positive role they could play in both providing low skilled work to the disabled and also how they could provide programs to help disabled Americans in their fight for independence. However, as UA demonstrates, the fight for independence is not just social. Some, if not much of the struggle, is psychological. It is a battle for freedom in our own minds. We must believe that even through this adversity we deserve to be independent. Even with these sweeping social changes, society was not willing to accept disabled citizens as having the right to freedom and movement. Today, even with an evolving American Disability Act, the struggle for full access and inclusion never ends. Perhaps our struggle will end only when we see ourselves as we want others to see us.

"Have faith in God," Jesus answered. "I tell you the truth, if anyone says to this mountain, 'Go, throw yourself into the sea,' and does not doubt in his heart but believes that what he says will happen, it will be done for him. Therefore I tell you, whatever you ask for in prayer, believe that you have received it, and it will be yours." -Mark,11:22-24

You can access much information from the ADA Web site. On the next page are a couple of general questions answered with the ADA act.

As technology progresses, and as more disabled people mentally overcome their challenges and take on the workforce, there will be greater and greater improvements upon our accessibility and mobility.

- If you are not disabled, do you know anyone that is?
- Can you empathize with this person knowing they want more from their life?
- Is there something you can do to help? Perhaps even following ADA legislation?
- If you are disabled, are your needs being voiced? Are you taking an ACT stance instead of a SAT stance?

In this chapter, we have reviewed the difference between physical and spiritual warfare, stated how important God is to your struggle, isolated your biggest issues, and asked some tough questions.

Are you prepared to continue this journey?

If so, let us look a little closer at your own individual needs and where I started to get where I have arrived.

Chapter Two
Defining Your Strikes

London Bridge is falling down, falling down, falling down. London Bridge is falling down, my fair Lady.

Build it up with iron bars, Iron bars, iron bars. Build it up with iron bars, my fair Lady.

Iron bars will bend and break, Bend and break, bend and break. Iron bars will bend and break, my fair Lady.

Build it up with gold and silver, Gold and silver, gold and silver. Build it up with gold and silver, my fair Lady.

Silver & Gold – Kirk Franklin & Family

We Fall Down – Donnie McClukin

Need we delve more into the history of African Americans in America, or the subservient role of women in America, or of the discrimination and misunderstanding of the disabled? After all, many reading this book already know these are real issues. With dozens of acts of Congress on the record covering each of the above topics there can be zero argument about the reality that these discriminations exist.

We certainly will continue to talk about these issues throughout the book. My life is dedicated to opening these issues to society and throwing challenges at them whenever I can. However, my argument is not solely about these issues.

Because you have issues, or strikes, that might reach outside the scope of my own issues.

My argument deals not so much with the reality of these social ills. My argument needs to convince you, the one dealing with life in the face of adversity, that there is a way out. Not just a way out, but also a way through. I have to show you a way to live so that society has no control over your mental well-being.

In the early 1950's when Rosa Parks took her place in the front of a bus, the majority of society told this woman she had no business there. But pockets of the world, even pockets of the South, told her she did have a right to sit in the front of the bus. She had the right to sit wherever she wanted. That mentality, well ingrained in her mind, made taking that seat no different than if we wanted to sit on a park bench today. Once we believe we deserve total inclusion, we will put ourselves in situations where we are included. Should our presence cause others to feel uncomfortable then perhaps we too can start social change. Those white men and women that heckled and threatened Rosa had no idea the historical significance of that moment. She might not have realized it either. After all, she was tired and probably needed to sit right then and there. It was a powerful mental decision on her part that will be taught and discussed for generations to come.

· What mental blocks are in your way?

· What, at this moment, would you consider your
   personal strikes?

· What is you think you aren't allowed to do that you
would love to do? Is there a way you can do it?

We are not human beings on a spiritual journey. We are
spiritual beings on a human journey. -Stephen Covey

Current studies show women earn less than men in equal
status jobs. On the other hand, women are outpacing men in
graduation rates (especially advanced degrees), and many
experts believe within a decade about half of the nation's salary
decisions will be made by women. How did this trend take
place? Mind over social expectations. But how will these high-
powered women perceive those in less educated circumstances?
What about the woman who still depends on an elevator to take
her from the corporate lobby to the secretary desk on floor 22?
Do we, as disabled women (or men or children) believe we
deserve that desk on floor 22? On the other hand, do we deserve
to start that small business of which we have dreamed? Do those
female CEO's believe we, as disabled bodies, deserve to run
major corporations? I suspect they too have discriminations of
their own to deal with.
   · How many people do you know that claim to be open-
     minded and yet you sincerely know they have biases of
     their own?
   · Do you have biases against a certain race or person?
     Are you African-American with biases against white or

Hispanic people?

· How can you work to break down those biases?

One theory is that capitalism (and this is a Marxist theory) will never allow for those without power-potential to join the ranks of the 'deserving.' Meaning, even if a minority of women reaches the stratosphere of the corporate ranks, even if they someday hold the majority of CEO ranks, there will always be the mindset of subservient roles. How many women today have had female bosses or supervisors that looked at everyone below them on the organization chart as less than equal? Even if women take lead roles in academia, business, and political positions, the idea of subjugation will still exist.

What then do we do? We cannot depend upon social norms to change. We must change ourselves into ignoring these social roles and putting ourselves into situations where we bust the glass ceiling and advance to our own potential.

We must take responsibility for ourselves and for those around us. Only then can we determine our own potential. Only then can we give strength to those around us helping lift them to where they want to go. Once in our history journalists questioned whether black Americans could survive without guidance of the government or an "owner." We dare not ask those questions today. So why must we accept the notion there will always be subservient mentality? It might be a theory, but our country has blasted theories apart for decades.

This is the main role of the University of Adversity. These steps will take you to a mental point where you can break through any societal expectation. You have to accept who you are. You have to decide what you can do and what you want. Then you have to get it. Nobody else will get it for you.

I did it. You can do it.

Alone or with support of loved ones around you, you must do it. You must take yourself to the level you deserve. This creed is for African American sisters in every city and burg nation-wide. But share the convictions with us no matter your background or ethnicity.

For All My Sisters, -Denotra Wallace

What makes me strong? My heritage.

What makes me weak? My fears.

What makes me whole? My God.

What keeps me standing? My faith.

What makes me compassionate? My selflessness.

What makes me honest? My integrity.

What sustains my mind? My quest for knowledge.

What teaches me all lessons? My mistakes.

What lifts my head high? My pride.

What if I cannot go on? Not an option.

What makes me victorious? My courage to climb.

What makes me competent? My confidence.

What makes me sensual? My insatiable essence.

What makes me beautiful? My everything.

What makes me a woman? My heart.

Who says I need love? I do.

What empowers me? My God.

Who am I? I am an African-American Woman.

I am Special: What is in a Name?

How many times have you heard the term 'special' used in regard to disabled Americans? It's a term used to place a bunch of different disabilities into one big pile. A person with severe retardation might be grouped with a mild stage of Spinal Muscular Atrophy (symptom appears only in limited ability to walk) and these extremes of 'special' might be matched in education or social assistance. In much the same way an Ivy League graduate might be separated from a Community College graduate, our society loves to keep people in boxes.

Thank God for God. His definition of special separates us only by DNA. And again, thank God I don't put people in boxes based on their fortune of attending such and such a school or having to work more or less than others to achieve what they have. Truth is, at the end of the day we are only standing before God and it is in His eyes we earn the status of Special.

Therefore, you are already there. Trust in that. Trust that you are not special because you can or cannot walk. You are special because you are a creation of the Creator.

Doctors considered me special and they wanted me to keep myself separated from the pack. My Nana considered me special in the way God considers me special, and she threw me into the pack to see myself as they see me. I cannot imagine my life if we had all just given in to what the doctors advised. I guarantee you would not have this book. I probably would not have a degree. I suspect I would be quite depressed.

Think of the names we give people to elevate or separate them from the pack. Lady Di was elevated by that title. Aretha Franklin because of her devotion and brilliance in musical performance is designated Queen of Soul. In African culture, those with the title African Queen were set apart as sovereign and supreme. In fact, many African American men refer to their women as their queen for this very reason.

What is a real elevated name? What is the ultimate in sovereignty?

The name above all names. The One that designates you and me as special apart from all worldly design. This name is promised to us to be the one name by which all our requests should be made known.

The Name Above All Names

There is joy in His name.

There is power in His name.

There is Peace in His name.

There is Love in His name.

Take these four statements to heart. No matter what your circumstance, there is joy in His name. Once you have come to the point of feeling no joy, through Him you will find it. Once you reach a point where you think society has claimed your stake in life, know you can reclaim it because through Him there is power. When everything seems to fall apart and life seems hopeless, there is peace. Most of all there is love.

Through Him, there is hope. Embrace this as a student of UA and you will soar to the top of the class. Remember, our classroom is our life, our day-to-day existence, and in that we can find joy, power, peace, and love. We must. Otherwise, these social arbitrary taboos will rule our day to day.

Why do I discuss spiritual issues through this book? Because you want to know the answers I found to overcome them. And the One with more names than society could ever create for me (black, negro, handicapped, lesser gender, "special") made me to be greater than all those labels.

He is called Immanuel (God with us), Beloved Son, Teacher/Rabbi, Son of Man, the Stone, King of Israel, The Word, Prophet, Lamb of God, Messiah, Bridegroom, Savior of the World, Bread of Heaven, Light of the World, Resurrection and Life, Truth and the Way, Prince of Life, Servant, Lord, Deliverer, Mediator, Shepherd, Alpha and Omega, Bright Morning Star, Faithful and True One, Advocate, and so many other names the Bible uses to describe Him. One of my favorites is the Great Physician.

However, because our physicians were subservient to His wishes for me, I walked, I talked, and I overcame their expectations because I believed in His outline for my life, more then I did theirs for my life. That is why this is a book and a course that requires a certain amount of faith to overcome your social stigmas. You do not have to agree, but I have no reason to think otherwise about the miracles of my life.

It is all a battle day in and day out. Even through the four truths above there is no substitute for standing ready against our spiritual and our real enemy. Keep in mind the enemy is not a race but rather something called ignorance. To bring knowledge to the ignorant we must first realize we ourselves are worthy. Then, we must battle the ignorant.

· What role do you feel God has in your life?

· Where else in your life have been able to find real, unwavering hope?

· What is your favorite title given to any historical figure? What is your least favorite title?

Military Might

During initiation into UA, you should think of your task ahead in terms the military uses. You have heard the phrase "Be All You Can Be," often used by the Army as a recruiting technique. Well, why should the Army have a monopoly on such a powerful ideal? With or without a uniform and physical weapon you can still be all you should be day in and out. Think of the landscape between knowledge and ignorance as a battlefield. Once I accepted who I was, the daily trials seemed like a battlefield in convincing not only myself but also others of my validity and usefulness. I became a warrior. The battle was for truth. The battle was and is for rights. The battle has put us all on an equal playing field. So, consider UA your boot camp and your basic training. It is not easy, it is sometimes very difficult, but it is necessary. If you think you have no hope, here is hope.

If you are mightily against war, that is okay. Nobody should like to see the carnage of a war. However, in our case we still must fight a war, as it is the only means of getting what we want. Of getting what we need.

Four Keys to God's Army
Be all you can be
Battlefield
Warrior
Boot Camp/Basic Training

Our task through UA is to make change happen even when our hands are off. By passing knowledge, we pass change into those who were once ignorant. We ACT, so there will be no SAT. Two issues we must address before we go further.

One is telling a little more about Nana, the woman that passed knowledge on to me. The other is passing on the information Nana passed to me: That without God we are without.

I Love Lucy

My Grandmother you might say saved my life. I do not know if I would have died without her, but I do know I might have. I might have given up. I do not know because I do not have to question this what if. In fact, Lucy Mae Cole was right in making sure I never forgot who I was or that I was a child of God.

Lucy was the mother of nine children, over thirty grandchildren and many great grandchildren. She lived a challenging, but blessed life. She was the soul of the family as well as the moral standard. She gave advice, and provided physical sustenance. Her permeating faith and beliefs were passed to family members. She was married to Henry Cole. My grandfather was a loving, hard working, and strong willed man. However, like most families, many of Lucy's challenges came by way of husband and family. Unlike many families today, they agreed to struggle through the tough times together. During times of health emergencies, food shortages, money, lack of parenting by children, homelessness of children and in times of children needing a babysitter, Lucy was right there. She was the spiritual leader. She was a pillar of salt for family and friends. She was my pillar.

During her lifetime, she was stricken with cancer, but through it and up until her final day the Lord provided her peace and comfort. Because she believed in the four steps mentioned earlier, steps essential to the UA, Lucy made it through even the most challenging of trials. In some way Lucy survived death.

Lucy Mae Hinton Cole stands at the top of the ladder of the epitome of the role of a mother and grandmother. "Precious is the death of a Saint in the eyes of the Lord." If the world could only receive a teaspoon of her being, faith and love, many lives would be changed. She was the opposite of, and her faith was an answer to, envy, strife, and hatred. She wanted the best to be better. She was my light out of the darkness.

Breaking the Cycle of Stages

What Lucy taught me above all else was to think positive of others and myself. We can set ourselves up to repeat cycles, to repeat mistakes, and wonder why life never changes. On the other hand, we can recognize and break these cycles. For a time

I repeated mental cycles that kept me in "my place." Especially when I was young.

In junior high, after fighting to get out of all of my remedial classes, I went to my level in everything except math. I was below my grade level in the course, but by eighth grade, I was in eighth grade Algebra. I broke the cycle that was expected of me. In my seventh grade English class, there were about thirty students. I deliberately chose to sit in the back of the class. My teacher called on me one day and said, "Just because you're sitting in the back doesn't mean that I don't see you." To break this cycle, in eighth grade English, I sat in the front of the class. I voluntarily raised my hand more and my teacher seldom called on me.

Doctors told my mother that I would never walk or talk; yet I walked in every one of my graduation ceremonies (junior high, high school & college). When I was nine or ten years old, at Matheny, I got out of my chair and stood up against the wall. I asked the attendant "if she could tell that I was handicapped." I do not remember her reply, but I refused to fall into these cycles expected of me. For one, my family never saw me the same way others did. Two, I knew if I did what was expected of me by society, the predictions of what doctors said I would become would be true. Moreover, I could not allow that to happen.

I made choices, goals, decided what I wanted, and figured out how to get there. Of course, I did not do it alone. I had the backing of many friends and God I trusted. I had family.

However, none of those people could force me to do any of this once I grew up. God always left it up to me to change my life he simply showed me the way. I had to ACT and make choices on my own. There was no other way for me.

[God says], do not fear, for I am with you; do not be dismayed, for I am your God. I will strengthen you and help you; I will uphold you with my righteous right hand.
- Isaiah 41:10 (New International Version)

Be Who You Are

In defining your personal strikes, you must be honest with yourself. List everything you can think of for which people judge you. Then, circle those things with which you might agree. It will not be fun, but adversity is not fun. That is why you are here. Once we get to the bottom of your strikes, then we can pull you through the University. My strikes were three main topics (African American disabled woman), but believe me when making a list of small things I had more than three strikes. However, these were the main strikes. After you make your list and are honest with yourself, then you can generalize them. Try to get down to your main strikes and those are what we will deal with through the book.

As you make this list, remember to be honest with both yourself and those around you. Make a list of perceived items. At the end of this book, you can feel free to burn this list.

Nobody needs to have a list of negatives sitting around to drain your energy. By the end of this book, you might not feel that list is such a negative list, though. We are going to try to turn into your curriculum of things to overcome and deal with in the University. There is no reason you should not feel that either this list can be faced straight ahead or that these traits/strikes do not really exist.

When you finish the list (and you should before you get to this paragraph) take a few moments to consider each point. Those that you have not circled consider if you think they are real or imagined. Really, consider them. If you decide they are not real, put an 'X' through them and get them out of your head. Next time you consider them, remember that big 'X' over the item and remind yourself they are not real.

The remaining points on the list are those we will think about through the rest of the book. First, read over the remaining list and put a 1), 2), and 3) beside the top three strikes against you. Those are your 'Major' topics. The rest we will deal with, but the main three are your three strikes.

Overcoming

Think of all those women in recent history that have overcome. Think of those in the throes of public eye right now; those watched while outsiders wait for their first mistake. We all make mistakes and we will all continue to make them. The important thing is how you deal with yourself. In the Bible, there are more women characters than meet the eye; Eve, Rahb, Ruth, Ester, Miriam, Bethsheba, Jezebel, Deborah, and Naomi.

They all lived in a culture that treated women not only as subservient, but also as lesser beings. They could be legally tortured and abused. Yet, many of these women became powerful and played important historic roles in world and biblical history. They overcame these cultural biases because, for most, their faith and beliefs were stronger than any label slapped on them.

Your list is a list of potential drains on your mental and physical success. It is possible you have not accomplished much in your life simply because of the things on your list. When I say accomplished, I do not necessarily imply monetarily. Perhaps you do not have the social life you desire. You might not have many hobbies or outside interests. You might need to exercise more. You might need to develop more educationally or culturally and you have never taken the steps to do any of the above. Maybe you do not know why. The reason could be the list.

Let us work on that list. Let us get it under control so it no longer controls you. Look at those top three strikes again. Can you see how number one might be the reason you cannot get the exercise you need because you think you do not deserve decent health? Has number two kept you from joining a club or social group? Has number three prevented you from getting out and taking a cooking class or dance lessons?

Life is too short to let a list keep us from doing all we want to do. You deserve whatever your heart seeks. No matter what your age is, or your social position, or what town you live in, there is a way out. There is a means of overcoming that list.

Think of those negative connotations around the word 'black.' Blacklisted, black sheep, the stock market crashed on Black Monday. Good grief! No wonder people question the importance of February as Black History month. For one, it makes February sound worse than it already is. Is there a more dreary and unusable month than February? I am sot sure we can change the negative connotation of how the word 'black' is heard as a negative. However, let me remind you that our race has endured much worse than verbal connotation. Our ancestors overcame physical and mental abuse, and we have it within us to overcome a simple overtone. In fact, we welcome the challenge. Because every obstacle we overcome builds character, and strong character is what makes for a life lived and fulfilled. The class ceiling established for women and African-Americans can be shattered. For those with a disability, the challenge is greater. But once we take the UA classes to heart, I believe we will ignore all these social stigmas. Once accepted we will believe in ourselves, we will believe we can overcome the strikes against us. We will soar like the eagles.

Chapter Three
Going a Little Further

My humanity suffered over my disability. Internally, I suffered. I saw all around me people with chances, options. Even in the African-American community, some were 'making it.' I wanted to be one of those that made it not by having it given to me, but by deserving and earning it. But how could I? How could I, with a disability, get out and earn anything for myself?

I would sit and watch people run to and from school, work, and the homes of their friends. I tried to wish away my disability. I tried to push it away with everything within me. Desperately at times, I cried out that if God could heal cancer, if God could make the dead live, if God could and had moved a mountain why would not He move mine? Why would He not reach down and touch me with His hand so I could be made whole?

My three strikes held me down. You might say, "Well, yes those strikes did. But look at you now."

This is my point. Looking at me now is proof that my list could not prevent me from rising to whatever I wanted. Keep in mind too that I am not done.

Life is a series of small hills that we climb. Even when we reach our first goals (and we will discuss goals later), we still need to make new goals. Eventually we wake-up and realize we are living a life far different that we ever expected. Most importantly, we have reached the basic goals for overcoming our main three strikes. New strikes are always going to appear and we must deal with those in the same way we deal with our overarching strikes.

Before we begin to deal with individual lists, we should consider how we got where we are. Why do we have strikes? In addition, why can we not just will them away? Why does God not just take them out of our lives?

For I am mindful of the plans I have for you, says the Lord, plans for your good and not for evil, to give you a future and a hope. You call upon me and come and pray to me, and I heed you You seek Me and find Me: Now you seek Me with all your heart and I am at hand for you, says the Lord...
  - Jeremiah 29:11-14a; Matthew 7:7

Unanswered Prayers

I learned a lesson about God. I believe He hears everything. I believe He hears everything we do, everything we ask, everything we want I believe God knows. However, our understanding is not His understanding. Do not confuse unanswered prayers with unheard prayers. Sometimes the "un-answering" is our answer. What we confuse for a God that does not listen is more often a God that does not grant for our own good. We need to know the difference between prayer and faith.

Prayer- The request according to our own will.

Faith- The act of belief that God is in control and His will shall be done.

Our prayers are requests according to our will. God takes these requests and fits them in according to His will for our life. Prayers are not unanswered, but rather granted only within the confines of the big picture of our lives. God knows the beginning, middle, and end of our lives. He knows what we can withstand and what is within our reach to overcome.

If you have issues you believe are unfair, trust that God has a means of making them both fair and a part of your life. It is not an easy step. It is tough to trust that what keeps us from "normal" behaviors are actually going to work in our favor. Moreover, perhaps you do not have strikes that put you in handicapped parking or keep you away from large crowds. Perhaps you just wonder what, overall, God has done for you.

You know what I learned? God entrusted me with these three strikes because He knew with patience and maturity my character was strong enough to make a difference. It could be that I was given these three strikes (in the eyes of the world) because I could handle it for His glory. I could handle overcoming through the University of Adversity because my character was strong enough. Maybe God has given you a perfectly normal life but for some reason you are feeling like this book is for you because you are thinking there must be more. You think that there must be more than just a day-to-day existence. Why does God not put a little pizzazz in your life? It all goes back to character. We must build ourselves into what we want to be. God will help us along the way.

Character- who we are based on the choices we make.

On the way to Calvary, Jesus went through Gethsemane. In Gethsemane Jesus found fertile ground for prayer. A parallel can be made between the olive trees that must be pressed for the oil and the pressing we go through to be made what we must become to handle what is in our path. Our Gethsemane is preparation and our praying ground. Let it be where you make your requests to God with faith enough to say "Not my will but yours, Father." What is the greatest unanswered prayer? Perhaps just before the cross, when Jesus said, "Father, take this away." However, God did not take it away because Jesus had to follow through with the will of God. And so Jesus also prayed, "Father, not my will but yours be done." He taught us that some prayers would go unanswered. He taught us we do not always know God's will for us, but we must trust that His will is greater than ours.

· What do you consider your greatest want that God has
   not granted?
· What do you think could be positive about this want
   not being met?
· Consider thanking God that in your time this need has
   not been met, but trusting in His time it will.

When you are being pressed God is still the Father.   The
relationship is not changed.

It is On the Way

Sometimes prayers go unanswered because we might have
the wrong motive. Expecting God to come through is easier to
talk about than to live out. Wait for the blessing with faithful
expectation.

Prayer is real. Ask God to test us, and He will bless us.
Moreover, through this faith of trusting the unanswered prayers,
we gain strength.

*God is there another way to handle this struggle? If so,
please reveal it.*

Once God hears your plea for understanding and clarity,
your path will be made known. You will walk forward in

confidence. Two more keywords you should take from this lesson are **Patience** and **Maturity.**

Patience will allow you to understand your requests are not being ignored, but are answered according to your big picture.

Maturity, both spiritual and practical, will come as you make choices and build your character.

I was once consumed with my own will being done. When I wished in desperation for my own will, I had no concept that God's will was more important. When we pray for His will, we are able to make choices in confidence that God will make our way, in His time, through our patience and growing maturity.

What if I had given up on God? He still would not have given up on me.

Therein lays the secret to faith. Trust that God is not going to ever give up on you. When the nurse dropped me on my head as a two-day-old child, the doctors gave up on me. The Doctors, mind you. Those with the knowledge from years of study, the experts, and the people trusted with our health and well-being. By no means do I disdain doctors. However, they said I would not make it and God knew better. They said I would not walk and God knew better. My grandmother said I would do what I wanted to do and I did because she had faith that could move mountains.

I first thought my mountain was my disability and unless my disability was gone, I had failed. However, my mountain was my disbelief. My mountain was my insecurity in myself. My mountain was the world telling me I needed to stay out of the way. I moved that mountain. My Faith through God moved that mountain.

Again, we will discuss goals a little later. However, I want you to start thinking in terms of goal making.

In order to overcome what God has put before us we need to rethink how we think about those obstacles. Then, we need to consider them part of who we are. Then, we need to convince ourselves that God put that obstacle there for a reason. At this point, we move into the goal-making portion of our lives. Before you continue through this book, it is important to understand the differences in faith and patience, goals and obstacles, and adversity versus imagination.

Who are you that you should be afraid of a man who should die and of a son of man who shall be made of grass? Do not be afraid of their faces; for I am with you to deliver you.
    - Isaiah 51:12; Jeremiah 1:8

Around the Corner

God has wisdom beyond our wants. He can see beyond what I am asking. God has purpose beyond our preferences.

Sometimes the mountain is time, patience. In addition, if we have faith in that patience, we will eventually round the corner and see what God has always known for us. The Bible says if we ask we shall receive. Notice that is does not say we will receive exactly what we ask for. It says if we petition God then we will receive from God. The Psalmist wrote that if we commit ourselves to the Lord and ask in faith, these things would come to pass.

The greatest miracles are not when God answers specific requests when our will matches His, but the great miracles are when we ask God to show the way and He does and it's more than we could have asked in our wildest dream. God has freedom beyond my request to be God and He will be God. He will do what fits for us in the big scheme. Trust God's wisdom, He can see around the corner, He is the beginning and the end. He is more experienced than we are and knows more than we know. God has a plan for your life. If God were to grant our every little request, it could cancel out The Big Picture.

We do not know tomorrow but we know our today. God knows our forever.

He knows if our little requests are granted that do not fit into our big picture, then we will not get the best He has for us. We must trust in His best for us. We must believe through patience and maturity in His will. Unanswered prayers are answered in His time.

Do not be discouraged. When my faith is most challenged, it is because my patience is being tried. I am not a patient person, and perhaps that is why I have to wait so often for so many things. It is a lesson I still have to learn. However, through patience we learn God's will for us. We see His path.

Disbelief

What about those that do not believe? How easy must it be to take God and throw him away when you cannot walk and He does not seem to be making it any better? Alternatively, when you cannot see, or you cannot hear, or you feel depressed because you are not the model on television or as wealthy as the businessperson ignoring you when he struts by? Easy to believe God is not there. It is simple to lose faith. However, through faith its how we reach our goals.

· What good does disbelief do you?

· Will you gain more by disbelieving than through the faith that God is guiding you along a path that He knows?

If God grants the small stuff, it might cancel the big stuff. Trust in the 'big stuff' for your life. There is no easy answer to this dilemma that has challenged men and women even in the days God walked Earth. When God stood before them healing the dead, when God spoke through a burning bush, when He arose three days after He was killed, people still doubted. It is easy to disbelieve in troubled times because we want so desperately for God to take away our pain or our weakness.

We need him to come to us and heal us. We need Him to show us His existence. Many disabled are disbelievers because they feel they have been ignored or punished. Once you come into the University of Adversity, you come in faith that God is leading you along a path of life.

Paul did the work of God. He talked about God, he taught, he preached, and he lived what God had him live. He was a living example. He fought the good fight, he ran his course, and he became the man God meant for him to be. Did Paul have moments of doubt? Certainly. However, they were short lived in the face of all the assurances Paul was given regarding his faith and his life. The Word will give you perspective and help reach your potential. Paul used the Word as his guide through all his adversity, confusion, and even when he was punished for his beliefs.

Paul was a forgiving person to those who opposed him. He went about his duties and his life as God wished and asked, and Paul was rewarded spiritually and physically. What we can learn from Paul is even when we are given reasons to disbelieve; we must maintain the course in faith. Some say he was a disabled or disfigured man. Even with potentially low self-esteem, Paul kept his focus on the Prize and went forth with confidence in the abilities God gave him. Do not feel guilty for the moments you are tempted to throw in the towel, but equally do not give in to that guilt. It is okay to doubt. It is not okay to let it linger. Overcome it with confidence through faith.

· Do you doubt the existence of God?
· How has your relationship to God been this week, the past year, and your life?
· Do you want to come back to God to help through your adversity? (Alternatively, strengthen your current relationship with Him?)
· How can you do this right now, before you continue? Take a moment just to thank Him for one thing in your life. You will be readied to move forward.

...do not fear, for I am with you; do not be dismayed, for I am your God.

I will strengthen you and help you; I will uphold you with my righteous right hand.

- Isaiah 41:10 (New International Version)

Ubontu

Ubontu is African Wisdom: *I Am Because We Are.* It is a statement of purpose and of solidarity. It is a recognition that one cannot go alone. It is important that God go with us. However, it is equally important that we not go alone amongst people. Am I speaking only of solidarity between African-Americans? I am not.

When I walked across that graduation stage in 8th grade, I used a loft-strand crutch (crutch that clamps around your forearm) on my right hand and a friend named Madeline held me with my left hand. In the middle of the ceremony, they called my name in recognition of having made the honor role every year of my junior high career. Madeline did not know this little secret about me and was quite surprised when my name was called. I gave her a knowing smile and we started across the stage.

She held my hand as I did what the doctors promised us I would not do. I walked across the stage. I needed her to help me across and along the way I needed the help of others. However, I also helped others. Madeline is a white girl. But our friendship went way beyond racial lines. We were friends because our hearts were the same. Our love was the same. She helped me across the stage and I like to believe in many ways I helped her as well.

Ubontu, African wisdom, reminds us that we cannot go it alone. Someone must help us (you) along the way. You cannot make the journey by yourself. Not the journey across the stage (teachers, parents, friends all help) and you cannot make the journey through life alone. More than any of this, you must allow God to help you through this journey as well. What you are helps those around you become who they are.

We all feed off one another. My friends and family helped shape me in a positive way. Surround yourself with positive people. Let them help you through your adversity and you in return help them. We all need that positive influence. It is recognized as far back as social studies have been conducted. What you are helps me to be what I am. What you are helps others to become what they will be.

If you are a positive influence, others will be better for it. If you are a negative influence, others will be worse for it. What God gives to us is for the good of others. We are to spread the light of our love and faith. By spreading our lights, we spread goodness the world round.

· List three people that can be your support system.

· List three people you can serve in a support role.

· What can you do for those three people today? Before the end of the week?

· What can you do for a complete stranger via a volunteer group or a charity?

Imagine that moment when Madeline helped me across the stage. Think of the people in that auditorium who in one moment saw how a disabled girl could make the honor role every semester and at the same time saw a white girl help a black girl across the stage. This was not a time in our history when different races often socialized. Things are a little better today, but not entirely healed. In fact, sometimes it seems racial understanding goes backward instead of forward on all sides of the issue. However, it must not be a factor in your life to get through this adversity.

Diversity is not a reason for division. Gifts from God are not color based. These gifts you should spread are not given based on race, ethnicity, age, or education. They are of God simple and plain for no other reason than giving gifts to others. It is not about your ability, but about God's love.

God does not give us leftovers, hand-me-downs, or useless, discarded, second-class gifts. He gives us the original gift created just for us to be used just by us. If we do not hold up our end of the bargain then our gifts are hidden from a world that needs those gifts.

I will cause you to walk in the straight way... I will open to you the gates of righteousness. For whoever find Me, finds life
- Psalm 118:19; Proverbs. 8: 35-6

Identity

We all have something that makes us unique. It is important that we use these the way God meant for us to use them. First, you must recognize them. What can you do that is unique to you? Sometimes it is a friendly word or handshake. Other times it is a job or task that needs fulfilled. Sometimes, it is offering volunteer work. Showing how you are overcoming adversity is also a means by which you can show your light. Yes, we have DNA make-up that genetically keeps us apart from others. It is our unique identifiable trait. However, while it separates us in many ways it is also a unifying marker because we all have it. Every living human (and other living beings) have their unique DNA structure.

This diversity is also a Oneness through God. He is our Creator, our stamp of approval, and through Him, we are all the same. God created black same as He created white. The sameness is a result of the Source (God). Diversity lies in the expression (how we conduct ourselves). We create diversity by choices we make. If you wear your hair up or down, color it black or pink, wear suits or jeans or skirts… all these factors create diversity. I was created different by my disability, certainly not my choice. I eventually embraced that diversity as my identity. I accepted it was who I am meant to be, it is me, and to have it otherwise would be taking away this diversity God wanted me to take part in.

Be who God wants you to be. Be an original. Do not be an imitation. Television, movies, and department stores would have us all look the same if they could (although they would right away start asking we begin changing). You should not make choices for yourself based on what the pop culture decides you should be. That is the point of originality: Becoming unique. So try it and take advantage of it. One of my favorite bumper stickers reads: "You Nonconformists Are All The Same." Trying to be original based on a fad or a spur of the moment idea is not originality. It is being a copycat. Be yourself, become comfortable in yourself, and in this you will be original. Then use those gifts you discover to help somebody so your life, and your living, won't be in vain. It is an amazing thing to help another person. Embrace this and you will have achieved much in this course of University of Adversity.

Be Who You Are

What kind of person does God use? We already talked about Paul. He was used by God in big ways. However, what if your goal is not to do anything similar to what Paul did. What if you want to succeed in business? Alternatively, be a prize-winning author, a top-notch teacher, a Nobel Prize winning scientist? Can you do these things and be who God wants you to be? Actually, if that is who are meant to be you cannot NOT be that person unless you fall inside the will of God.

God saved me both spiritually and physically in this world. He lifted me higher than I thought I could be lifted. He gave me more than I thought I could be given. It was an amazing transformation for me, and it was it taught me everything I needed to know to recognize the system of University of Adversity. Therefore, who would I be if I did not return the thanks? Who would I be to not give myself to be who God meant for me to be? How can I refuse to find out His will for me? If He wants to use me then I will be used graciously and gratefully. In addition, how can I refuse?

Not everyone can be used in the same capacity. However, once you know who you are through God then you can be used in your own capacity. Gideon was told by God that he was to lead his people from bondage. Gideon told God he was the least of all the people and was probably not the best choice. God's basic reply was, "If I choose you, you will be made more than able to lead your people." Moreover, because of Gideon's humility and willingness, God gave him a life beyond what Gideon thought he was able to live. We all have our abilities and if we fall into our role, even with hesitation, we can fulfill great needs. You can accomplish anything you set as a goal. In addition, more than this, if everyone sets out to change their own world, eventually it can change the entire world. Devote yourself to goodness and to honesty. Run the race before you.

There is no challenge not to be who I am. Running around pretending to be someone else (copying the television perhaps) is not a challenge. Actors have a tough job because they have to learn a script. However, without the script when they play someone else all they would have to do is walk around and pretend. If I lived my day-to-day life without a script and without an identity of my own, there would be no challenge. It would be easy. God does not want us to pretend to be someone else. He needs us to be who he designed us to be. Using our gifts and learning through our own adversity. There is a difference between character and reputation.

Character- *Who you are based on choices you make.*

Reputation- *Judgment based on others and what they think of you.*

Reputation is important, but character is what is real. However, the worst example of betraying your identity is to put on a false character to change your reputation. Trying to get people to see a you that do not exist is false identity. In addition, many people can see right through it. When we are trying to build our self-esteem, we must pay attention to living as our original selves and not as what we think people want to see. Positive behavior represents the best quality of who you are. Own up to who you are despite the temptation to be someone else. Do not fake your reputation according to what you think others want to see. Create a character you are proud of and your reputation will fall into place. No matter your character, is a positive example? Be who God created you to be. Shine.

Chapter Four

Purpose of the Pit

Just as I believe there are reasons prayers are not answered, I also believe there are reasons we are placed in moments of hopelessness. I am not suggesting we plan for hopelessness or even desire it. Life is about living it to the fullest. The fullest life is living a happy, productive existence full of love and kindness. Surrounded by hopelessness is not the most effective means of living out these ideals.

However, life is also a roller coaster ride. It is a world where we have moments of deep depression. It is full of times where we feel trapped. Now that you have taken the plunge into the University of Adversity, there is a harsh realization we must discuss. It is about honesty. It is about having the freedom within to explore and admit to our weaknesses and our fear.

In order to lay this out, we need to examine a character in the Bible whom God put into a fit of despair. A man with whom God gambled would not lose faith even in the worst of circumstances. Job had everything taken from him. His property, his family, his health. Yet, he did not lose faith. Did he have moments of doubt? Yes. Did he question why this was happening? Yes. However, it did not change the fact he was in a pit of despair.

There was a purpose. Part of the purpose was for God to prove there was a man of great faith left. However, for Job it was also a learning experience? Job learned that God is in control and that for God to allow all this punishment must mean that God would give insight about the nature of suffering at the end. In fact, Job was not only given this spiritual insight, but he was rewarded for his faithfulness. For him, the pit had multiple purposes. In addition, your pit also has multiple purposes. One of those purposes is not to lose faith.

Hungry and thirsty, their soul fainted in them. Moreover, he led them forth by the right way and filled their hungry soul with goodness.
- Psalm 107: 5-9

Reactions to the Pit

You can react to the pit positively or negatively. Probably, if you are like most, you will experience both reactions. However, one has to win out and that choice is yours. Your reaction to the pit leads to rescue from the pit.

Alternatively, it leads to your wasting away. As we mentioned earlier, you cannot do this alone. Sometimes you need a hand helping to pull you from the pit. In my case, it was the help of my family and friends, like Madeline who gave me a hand to do what I needed to do. Underlying it all I could have blamed God for my misfortune. In addition, sometimes I did blame or at least doubt. However, more than not, by encouragement of family, I trusted that God would be faithful. He is.

Take out a sheet of paper and answer the following questions before you continue forward. Remember, this does you no good unless you are completely honest with yourself. Answer these without editing yourself.

Nobody else is going to read these responses unless you request it. Nobody is going to know what you say or what your worst trials are.

Maybe you do not have any at the moment, but I suspect if you are reading this, you have a few pits of your own. You might not want to read anymore after this exercise, but take some time and think if you are leaving anything out. Then, come back to the University for more.

1) What is the greatest struggle in your life this day?
2) What was the most recent hurtful pit you have experienced?
3) Who helped (or is helping) more than anyone?
4) How comfortable are you talking to God about this?
5) Do you blame God (or question God) for this pit?
6) What do you need to help you out of the pit?
7) What happens if this pit gets deeper before it gets

better?

8) Name two things you can do this day to move forward
   in your struggle.

[God says,] "This rather is the practice that I wish: releasing those bound unjustly, untying the thongs of the yoke, setting free the oppressed, breaking every yoke, sharing your bread with the hungry, sheltering the oppressed and the homeless, clothing the naked when you see them and not turning your back on your own flesh. Then your light shall break forth like the dawn; your wound shall quickly be healed; your vindication shall go before you, and the glory of the Lord shall be your rear guard. Then you shall call and the Lord will answer." - Isaiah 58:6-9

It is Just a Test

You have listened to the radio when an emergency broadcast signal was relayed. Alternatively, the television when an annoying tone is emitted followed by an announcement that either this was a test, or there is some sort of emergency. Usually, it is a test of the emergency broadcasting system. "This is only a test." It is put into place in the event of a real emergency. Then, everyone would be prepared for that tone followed by a definition of the emergency and what to do next. It's a system set up on all radio and television networks nationwide. Some towns have their own siren system to alert citizens to various weather or town emergency situations. Again, the reason is so everyone knows the signal when a real emergency is announced. Everyone will respond in the same way.

God has this similar broadcasting system.

Some of what we go through is God's interruption to the normal progression of life's pilgrimage. God designed certain struggles to be a test. The small tests, whatever they may be, will end and life can return to normal. It might shake you up, but it will not mess you up. It might slow you up, but it will not throw you out of the game. God tests His children not to show your weaknesses but to show and encourage your spiritual strength. If you want to grow, you must be open to these tests.

You must persevere through these tests. You need to stand firm in your faith, hold tight to your friends, and ACT. DO NOT SAT these tests. You must move forward to a solution. You must move through your life holding to friends and striving to reach your goals.

Tests are designed for you to measure how much more of your life is under God's authority of faith than before. Sometimes we are tempted to give God a percentage of our faith. We say, "You get faith in these areas, but in others I'm not so sure yet so let's see how this goes." However, after you are tested, God opens more of your life to Him in faith. Perhaps you trust God in areas of family life, which you believe your family is protected. No matter what they are faced with, they will persevere.

However, perhaps you do not trust God in areas of finances. You are not quite ready to take risks you want to take because you have not turned that area of your life over to God. Tests and falling into financial pits will eventually show that you can then turn this part over to God in faith as well. It is all about facing these tests and risks head-on, without fear, with support, and with faith. You will come through on the other side a better person. You will learn to trust more in God. The adversity will eventually seem less taxing when faced with faith.

Run the race with patience. Press toward the mark. The race is not given to the swift or the strong, but the one who endures to the end.

The first command is to love God with all your heart and strength and mind.

The second command is like unto it: love your neighbor as yourself.

- Jesus

Broken to Whole

What might be one of the ultimate pits a human can endure? Perhaps complete loss of control over choices, family, jobs, sleep, food, or clothing. In a sense, the greatest pit a person can face is being owned by another, without rights, without the liberty to pursue any goals. Not just the goal of career or family, but the goal of taking a walk through a field or reading a book. Slaves were stripped of all these rights. Not just in the early American South or British/French slavery of Africa and other nations, but even today there are slaves in part of the world under dictatorships.

Think about all the control of your life literally stripped away and supported by the government so you have no choices. This is a pit. We discussed this toward the first of the book, but think about how the slaves came out of this. They sang. They created poetry, spirituals, sermons, and held as tight to God as any people ever have. The reward came, in time. Today in hymnals, church-wide congregations of all denominations sing these songs with weary-eyed boredom that were once songs that kept people alive. These songs made slaves trust that a better day was coming, that the Gospel Train would come, and that Grace was Amazing.

Jesus cares about our internal lives as well as our external. He works with us from the inside out. When we are broken, the deepest breaks usually take place inside. Our legs might not work, our eyes might quit, or our bank accounts might be empty, or job taken away, our partner leaves unexpectedly. These are external breaks. However, the real hurt is inside.

The wounds are deeper in our psyche, our souls, and our hearts. God can heal the external, but He is most interested in the internal. It is through the internal that we touch others. Our souls motivate us to great things. Our minds chart the course of decisions we make. These are the areas that, when wounded, can hold us down in the pit. We must let God heal the inside first. We must be willing to turn over the inner turmoil before we work on the external.

Sometimes we are tempted to say, "Once my finances are in control, then I'll be okay." "As soon as this disability is under control, then I'll move forward." "Once I have control of my life I'll feel secure." You cannot wait for the externals to heal before you move on. You have to work your way up and take control through faith, hope, and trust. Adversity is best overcome when ACTed upon, not waited upon.

Slaves do not get psychologists. They do not have mental health insurance coverage. They trusted in men like Isaiah who said, "He will keep then in perfect peace him whose mind is stayed on Jesus." During the days of slavery, they kept their minds on God. During my struggles, I keep my mind on God. During your struggles, you must keep your mind on God. It is the way through adversity.

Social Impact

Another argument for making yourself whole is something we will cover in depth later. However, I want to mention it here because one of our goals through the University is to reach others in the same situations we were once in. (Or will soon be out of.) The social impact of staying focused on God are incalculable. When you are the last choice and Jesus chooses you, all those people that once passed you without a glance will wonder why they missed in you what Jesus knew always existed. God brings out our best and shows it to the world. We cannot show it ourselves or we lose humility. However, once we focus and we show for God what God has done for us, we are in His will. Those around will not ignore us. They will embrace our positive attitude, they will embrace our faith, and they will embrace us when we embrace them.

When you weather the time in the pit, you do not fall when things around you do. Moreover, it is evident. It is a tool. An evangelistic tool and we will cover this later as one of the bonuses of being involved in the University of Adversity.

God expects us to be real. He wants us to have enough faith to believe we can be real for ourselves and those around us.

Can a woman forget her suckling child, that she should not have compassion on the son of her womb? Yes, they may forget, yet I will not forget you.

- Isaiah 49:15

Negative Impacts

What are some of the potential negative impacts? Depending upon how you react there are potential negative aspects. If you give up hope then you give up. People will see this.

Weakness shines when you throw in the towel and you show your faithlessness. It is not unheard of, and sometimes even the act of giving up is simply digging a deeper hole in the same pit. In addition, eventually you have to get yourself out anyway, but from a deeper place.

Another potential downside is lashing out and blaming others for your circumstances. Certainly, there are numerous times when the condition we are in is the fault of others. Slavery is an excellent example. Even then, the attitude was one of hope and not of conflict. Conflict in many situations only leads to more harm done.

The bottom line is to not put blame anywhere. What does blame do other than take responsibility off us? That only helps us feel better; it never solves the problem. Never.

Blaming others makes us feel less responsible for the situation, but it does not get us out of the pit. It is a temporary, useless band-aid. Nobody will be helped by blaming others, including ourselves. Be wary of lashing out, and understand that blaming others (true or not) does not lift you from the pit.

One of the most harmful and dangerous of all is the use of alcohol, drugs, or sex to alleviate the pain. Talk about digging deeper pits. These empty solutions create whole new issues. Moreover, the most dangerous side effect of all is becoming blind to the pit itself. You start to believe the pit is your new life. You feel at home here because you are intoxicated. You cannot see the solutions or even the problems. It is an easy and dangerous road to take.

You lose not only every chance of positive social impact, but you create a pit within a pit. You then have to someday overcome your dependence on the vice, and then you have to deal with the pit that got you there in the first place. Even harsher is losing perhaps years of your life you can never reclaim. This is a warning that if you have turned to these vices even on a surface level, get out of them now before you cannot see the new pit.

If you have found yourself buried in them, it is time to seek help. Call out to God to release you from these vices and then find a pastor or counselor to talk you out of the situation. Again, you should not try to do this alone. Find someone to walk with you across this stage of your life, and you will soon be back on solid ground.

The pit is a dark place. I was there as a child, I have been there as a woman. The University of Adversity, faith in God, will not release you from ever falling back into a pit. However, once you take these steps to confront your problems instead of ignoring them or blaming them on others; you will find the pit is really just a dip in the road. You can choose to react positively or negatively. You can choose to accept your personal responsibility for liberation from the pit (even if somebody else put you there) or you can choose to sit and waste away in self-pity.

God does not want us to be self-loathing or self-pitying. He is a God that wants people to look to us as examples of what faith can do. I am not suggesting by any stretch that you put on a false face. Do not pretend to be on a hilltop when you are living in the depths. That does you no good, others no good (because they will eventually find out), and it does God no good.

You must come to faith on real terms. If you are not there yet, or you still have so much anger that you are not ready to forgive God for your pain; that is okay. Hang on with me. In the next chapter, we will discuss how to liberate yourself, and how to rip yourself off. Moreover, the biblical David lived some of his life in a pit as well. I have more stories to tell, and we both have more lessons to ponder.

Chapter Five

Process of Liberation

We are going to discuss HOPE in this chapter.

HOPE- *Harnessing Optimism through Personal Experience.*

Living in a pit leads to hopelessness. In the last chapter, you took some time to consider what your pit is. What it is that keeps you from having hope? You might not have a vision for tomorrow. Or maybe your family is falling apart. Or your finances are a disaster with no easy solution. The number of hopeless situations are more than I can list here. The point is that you need something to lift you from the pit. Once you find your solution, what do you next? You hold on to hope and HOPE. You harness optimism not by seeing your pit as a negative, but by viewing it as a learning experience.

I know your pit might be something unimaginable to us. But you have a choice to see it as a negative, unwilling to let it go for your own good. Or you can choose to see it in such a way that you learn something even if that something is the fact you can weather storms. Use your personal experience as a means of harnessing optimism. This practice of HOPE leads to a brighter vision of tomorrow. Through my CP, I have learned more than I dreamed I would be able to learn and do. These lessons of climbing out of pits gives me the hope to move forward and try new things, take new risks, put together an outline for overcoming adversity. I have done all of these through a spirit of hope because of where I have been.

Earlier you made a list comprised of strikes and three of those strikes are your biggies. This is where we look at those biggies a little closer. In a moment, I am going to introduce to you four basic steps toward liberation. You can take a peek at them now in the table below. They are the means of dealing with your strikes. When you can embrace these four steps then you are ready to embrace liberation. It will not happen overnight as we will discuss.

Take your list of three and look at them again. Make sure they are your biggest strikes. Moreover, ask yourself again how you can see yourself being all you ever dreamed by overcoming these three adversarial points.

It helps to have a family of constant reminders, yes. However, most of my personal experience has been my guiding light. Once I learned to look back at the ugly times in a positive light, everything changed.

Four Basic Steps Toward Liberation
>Maturity
>Acceptance
>Self-Actualization
>Self Determination

We will discuss each of these steps below. Remember that these are steps toward liberation and that liberation is hope. Once you feel in control of your situation and your life, you are liberated. You are free to be who God meant you to be, and not the negative minded stranger even to yourself.

· Have you ever looked in the mirror and thought the person you meant to be is not looking back?
· Do you blame that on a disability?
· Do you blame the stranger in the mirror on social issues?
· Do you put the blame on your family or friends?

Not to beat a beaten point, but these are all destructive habits. If you do not take responsibility for your own mistakes, you will never reach the first step to liberation.

Maturity

The first thing that happens is you mature. I have met mature 18 year-olds and immature 50 year-olds. Maturity should come with age, and usually does, but it is not a promise. Maturity is how we look forward from where we have come. If the thought of a potential disaster wrecks havoc in your mind causing you to lose sleep, you aren't approaching life with as mature an attitude as someone who might be aware of potential disaster but still chooses to live for the day.

Maturity is gained through experience. It is an earned level of personality. As mentioned above, if you tend to blame others for the problems in your life, you lack maturity. Down to the smallest issue in the workplace...blaming others leads to a destructive mindset. We must take responsibility for our own lives. If we do not, we can never be who God wants us to be. We can never feel we are responsible for ourselves. We can never take control of our life.

Maturity is an outlook. It is an attitude of how things are faced and then how we act upon them. I could blame the nurse for my health issues. She is a trained professional and she dropped me; a baby, fragile, and she did in fact inflict harm on me. However, I had to deal with that. I had to move on. Why? Because it could not be undone.

We cannot talk about fairness because of course it was not fair. If I had lived my entire life up to this very day blaming her for my every misstep (and believe me, at times she did get much blame), I would not have taken my life into my own hands. I would perhaps spend afternoons groveling in self-pity, day after day, without anything. I would not have a degree, I might not have friends (or positive influences), and I would not have stood in the face of the naysayer and accomplished one thing. I might not be alive. I certainly would not be writing this book. Because if I had chosen to spend my life blaming my health on one person (even when the reality is someone is responsible for my condition), I would not have taken control of my life.

Rejoice and be glad...for the Lord God is your exceeding great reward.

   - Isaiah 66:10; Genesis 15:1

Acceptance

Acceptance is when we say, "Okay Diedra, this is the hand you've been dealt. Now then, what do we do today?"

I devised goals for myself. I wanted friends. I wanted a life outside of how I was viewed. I wanted to create myself. Did you get that?

I wanted to create myself.

I first had to accept that this is where I was, this is who I am, and this is what I have to work with. And you know I found there was a heck of a lot with which to work. I am still tapping into my own potential. However, before I could even detect potential, I had to accept where I was and who I am. This was the first and most important act of liberation. I soared from then. It did not happen overnight. One day you might decide you are happy in your own shell, your own condition, your own situation. Then the very next day wake up, look in the mirror and think, *This is not for me. I do not want to be this.*

You have got to grab hold at that point and ask the hard questions. You have got to dig deep. I am going to list more questions here but this might not be the moment to answer them.

Bookmark this page and on a day you are not feeling the acceptance of yourself, turn to this page and ask yourself the tough questions. Again, detailed honesty is the only way to approach this.

· What don't I like about myself? List them.
· Is there anything I can change, control, or make more acceptable to me (remember... we aren't asking what others find unacceptable... we are asking your opinion of you)? Beside the above list, list potential changes.
· What if I can't make these changes? Which of those items can't be changed? Can I accept that?
· Assume nothing from this moment on will change for you. What about yourself do you love? What are your strengths?
· How can each of those strengths listed be used to help reach every current goal for your life?

You see, by answering these questions realistically you reach a point where you realize you do have strengths. Those strengths, even with no other changes, can take you closer to your goals. With more acceptance comes potential for real change.

Self-Actualization

Once I reached a point where I could look in the mirror and accepted myself, loved myself, believed in myself, I had to define myself. This is a tough task, but a vital task. Realizing first what we have discussed to this point, you know you are a child of God. You know you are a person with a purpose. You know you have a task, a goal, a job to help lift those that are down out of their valley. However, how can you if you do not truly believe you can?

Experts say it takes 21 to 30 days to form a habit. Thinking of yourself in terms of having the ability does, in fact, require some habit forming. Again, you do not want to lie to yourself or become fake. You need to really believe, deep in your soul, that you are a child of God able and chosen to make an impact.

Take those strengths you outlined above and begin to define yourself by them. Use them daily and as you do your confidence will grow. It helps to surround yourself with positive voices outside your head as well as inside. My family and my friends were my constant source of encouragement. But not until I started listening to them did I realize their truth. It was one thing to have voices my whole life telling me I was worth more than gold. It was another to really hear those voices and tune into them. Once I tuned in, once I started believing those voices and internalizing what they said, the positive changes within began.

The positive voices countered all the negative voices from those that did not know me. Once I believed all they said, and learned I was worth even more than their words, I changed. I accepted myself and began to ask myself who I was. I learned I was an achiever with great potential. I learned I could take my differences and turn them into positives. Diedra was born in a new way and I embraced this 'me.' I made goals to complete my education. I made goals to make a difference in lives of others.

Self Determination

The fourth step to true liberation is taking all this and moving toward the accomplishment of your goals in the face of all adversity. This fourth step, once achieved, makes you a life-long participant in the University of Adversity. You are equipped to move forward with confidence because you have achieved the basic desire and irrefutable determination for success. We are not talking about financial or shallow success here. We are talking about walking day after day with intense purpose, definition, and life changing ability.

Do you remember the Bible story where a woman, a simple woman, asked Jesus what she could give to him? His response was that in willingness alone she had given much. Your willingness to reach this fourth point (and you cannot do it in a day) demonstrates the potential you have as a servant of God and a servant to fellow men and women. You realize, finally, that you are in a war zone and in your mind is the battlefield. God did not get you to this point only to leave you empty. You reach point four, after deep self-searching, and you are poised to soar like I soared.

Remember, those around you might not think you can soar. They might still try to box you up, tell you that you should not walk because you cannot walk, or tell you that you cannot do whatever it is they think you cannot do. Whatever box you are placed in, bust out of it at this point. Do not be transformed to this world because this world, this society, this reality is temporary.

What you are supposed to do at thirty not only changes by the time you are forty, but the next generation has different societal expectations on them. Point is, it all changes. Trying to fit into some temporary societal box is more robotic than human.

Fit into your own world, what you envisioned for yourself when you went through self-actualization. That is the you that you need to be, not what somebody else has defined you should be. And walk on with this thought in mind, a promise from God, that no weapon (words, ideas, stereotypes) formed against you shall prosper. If it cannot reach your mind, it cannot prosper. Only you can let it in to eat away at the positive changes you have made. No weapon can penetrate your stronghold. The weakness is in you alone.

Adversity is the diamond dust that heaven polishes its jewels with. - Leighton

More Than What You See

Here is the other lesson. While you build yourself into a person that overcomes adversity with skill and pizzazz, you need to be aware of your own judgment of others. What you see in others, especially on first encounter, is rarely what you get. Sometimes the person becomes even more intriguing and inspiring. Often, though, we are left disappointed.

That is okay. Because just as you hope they expect the best from you (though they do not always deliver), you should expect the best from them no matter what your first impression. If the person is a negative voice, then by all means turn the dialogue positive or walk away, but do not play that game again. If you have beyond blaming others, feeling lost, believing you are worthless, then do not let someone drag you back down. What you see may not be the whole story.

We are more than our titles. I am more than any degree I might be handed. I am my mother's daughter and a soul bigger than any handicap that can be placed on me. Others are more than what they might realize as well. When you meet that person who believes they are bigger than they really are, give them the benefit of the doubt. Sometimes those people are compensating for rough times in a different way.

Remember I said you should not be fake? There is a theory of thought asking people to 'believe' they are more than they are and yet they do not ask the hard questions. They do not delve deep. They do not live self-sacrificing lives in the humility of

God. They are still children of God and yet miss out on the joy of the Lord because they live in a false joy.

Your challenge in accomplishing liberation is to:

Reveal the mystery of what you will be...
Reveal the certainty of who you will be...

Maturity is what we strive for. We mature through experience and our reaction to those experiences. We mature by watching how those we respect respond to adversity. Or, we realize we might not be mature if we have no one in our lives we truly respect. We focus on the negative instead of the positive, and that is a sure sign of immaturity.

We move forward through acceptance of our situation. We stop blaming the world or others. We accept our situation and decide to move forward by finding those strengths within. We determine to make ourselves better by realizing who we truly are, and setting goals to become who we have the potential to become. Then, we move forward with determination and drive to our destiny.

Little by little we learn more, ever more. I have learned this book was within me, and I could never have reached this point without overcoming the demons inside my head. I am excited about tomorrow and what it will bring. The mysteries of who I am yet to become are still being revealed. What is my last chapter and what am I leaving behind?

The certainty of who I will become lies in my security that God is my God. I ask Jesus what I can give and in my willingness alone, He is pleased and he uses that daily. This is my determination: To let society think what it will of me and meanwhile be who God has made me. Often those are two different people. I can assure you, the Diedra that society once saw does not exist. She never existed. I believed she was me, but as it turns out my mother and Grandmother were right all along.

Chapter Six

Rip Yourself Off

This is kind of a harsh title, but easy for us to do. It was easy for me to do.

Life is about self-esteem and making choices that lead to good self-esteem. It is not enough to listen to those around you, even if you are surrounded by people that build you up. You have to give yourself credit. You have to be your own cheerleader, able to lift yourself when the going is tough. It does not matter what those around you say, (good or bad) when you are able to lift yourself out of the negativity.

Therefore, it is easy to rip yourself off. It is easy to forget that you are a child of God and worthwhile for that reason alone. When you cannot walk, when you cannot do what everyone around you can do, when you feel like nothing is going the way you want, it is easy to believe you are not worth much. That is taking away your right to live day after day believing in yourself. It does not matter whether we are talking about your ability to run a race or your ability to climb to the top of the corporate ladder. You are limited only by what is in your mind. You might not have the education to get where you want to go, but you can get that education. The education is not the limitation. Your mindset is what limits you from getting that education.

Here is what happens when you don't love yourself, accept yourself, or recognize your potential. You sit around and wait for life to happen. You drain those around you. Even more, you lose the day. You lose the day God gave you and the sun rises then sets and you have lost your day. You do not get that chance back and before long, you have lost your self. You lose out on all that you can be. You rip yourself off.

When my family encouraged me to pull it together and become something more than what I thought I could be, it was not that I entirely ignored them. I believed they were wrong. Not mistaken, not patronizing; I thought they were dead wrong.

"Diedra, you're gonna' make a difference."
"Diedra, you can do anything you want to do."
"People love being with you. You are special in many
  ways."
Nana wrote in my yearbook that "God doesn't make
  junk."

I heard these day after day but it never meant anything because I was cheating myself out of what was truth. I could have continued down this path. What would it have cost me? In a sense, everything I am I would not be. If you do not have these positive influences in your life, you should find them. Find them and listen to them. Let them be the voices until you realize their truth. Otherwise, you will never move ahead. You can never move forward. You can never find who God wants you to be because you will have lost yourself. You will cheat yourself. You will rip yourself off.

There are warning signs. If you do not love yourself, you are ripping yourself off. If you do not accept who you are, you are ripping yourself off. You have ripped yourself of a future if you do not love and recognize your potential. It is another tough series of questions and reaching into deep places. However, here we go because this is another part of University of Adversity course requirement.

It is not the critic who counts, nor the man who points out how the strong man stumbled, or where the doer of deeds could have done them better. The credit belongs to the man who is actually in the arena, whose face is marred by dust and sweat and blood; who strives valiantly; who errs and comes short again and again; who knows great enthusiasms, great devotions; who spends himself in a worthy cause; who, at the best, knows in the end the triumph of high achievement, and who, at the worst, if he fails, at least fails while daring greatly, so that his place shall never be with those timid souls who know neither victory nor defeat.   *- Theodore Roosevelt*

Not Loving Yourself

We touched on this in the last chapter. It is a vital point of change for you and for me. We must come to love ourselves. That is the positive aspect. Let us discuss the negative aspects.

In an earlier chapter, we talked about the Pit. Remember we discussed how falling into this pit means we need to learn to rely on others to get us out. However, if we do not think we deserve to get out, we will not ask for help. We will not let someone know we need that help. I did love myself. Not at first, not before I found out the steps to liberation. Therefore, I was stuck in the pit, alone, no help, nobody dropping a rope. I did not think I deserved that rope. I ripped myself off for years stuck in that pit, feeling hopeless.

King David, who rarely was accused of not loving himself, had a similar struggle when he considered himself in the eyes of God. David, in his own eyes, was a strong and respectable man. David, assuming to look through God's eyes, saw himself as unworthy and unloved by God. Yet his actions at times were self-destructive.

It was not until David saw himself through the eyes of God that he found a way to live that was respectable. When he loved himself as God loved him he began to do great things in the lives of those around him and for the nation. His initial self-love was not the same kind of love God wants us to have for ourselves. We are talking about a love for ourselves that if we forget to pay a bill we forgive ourselves. If we run over a neighbor's pet our inner voices do not accuse us of being lazy but rather just not the driver we should be.

If we lose our way in life, we trust that we will get ourselves out and not repeat over and over that we deserve this pit.

Our self-love is the key to our success. Think about all the negative things you feed yourself day in and out. When I suggest creating a more positive mindset, I am not suggesting you go into false voices that will eventually make you believe in yourself. I mean believe in yourself then those voices, real voices, will stay in your head because you have taken on a new view of your life.

It is one thing to love yourself. It is another to accept yourself. I do not believe you can accept yourself until you love yourself. However, you can love yourself and still not accept yourself. The difference, I believe love is in the purest sense. You can lose your limbs, you can get fired, you can lose a house, and you can lose your spouse. In the face of all this you still love who you are still wanting change but able to forgive. Forgiveness is a sign of love. It is a reflection of love. If you can forgive yourself of your actions then you have reached a level of love. However, you might still look in the mirror and say, "I don't like who I am."

Not Accepting Yourself

Ever been in love with someone and realize you don't really like them? It is a frequent theme in long-term marriages or relationships. Siblings suffer this. You forgive over and over, you would give your shirt for someone; but you do not really like them. Probably you once did like them. Then one day their smoking habit made you crazy. Or the way they laugh sends chills up your spine. Or their flipping through television stations makes you want to toss the remote through the television screen. That is dislike. That is not accepting who the other person is. It is the same way with ourselves. In fact, it is that times ten because the little things that bother us about us we deal with day in and day. It is separate from love and important to think of it this way.

When we face adversity, it is impossible to overcome that adversity unless we believe we deserve it. You will not feel you deserve it until you love yourself and you accept who you are.

If you take no other truth from this book, take this truth: God accepts you as you are. Your imperfections, your impurities, your moments of doubt are all in His radar screen and He 100% accepts you as you are. Why then are we so slow to accept ourselves?

Part of it, I think, is that we want to be more than we believe we can be. It is a circular problem. When I was in my low moments, I believed I was right where I deserved to be. Not because I was a bad person but because I was a conflicted person. I did not accept myself. Therefore, while I wanted more for my life, I did not think I could get there because I did not believe I deserved to get there. If I did not believe I deserved it, obviously I did not make strides towards improvement. What would the point have been? If I did not make strides, I never would have changed. This is circular reasoning.

My first realization came when for the first time I realized how God sees me. He sees me as I am at this moment and I am accepted. From there, I can accept myself. David got to the point where he accepted himself humbled before God. Job accepted both himself and situation, humbled and trusting in God. It is not enough to love yourself. You also must like yourself.

You are sitting in a coffee shop or a café. Someone walks by and smiles or nods. You are going to have different reactions to this depending on your opinion of yourself. You probably do not trust the positive aspect of it. On the other hand, you take it too far and think the person is in their own right distrustful. You wonder why they acknowledged you. Is it because you are black and you felt it was a pity nod? Is it because you are handicapped and it was a sympathetic nod? Have you ever, on first reaction, thought "What a nice person" and then return the gesture? Probably rarely. Why?

Because we need to think that first the person cannot be seeing us in a positive light if we are not seeing ourselves that way.

To like those around you, including strangers who show a moment of kindness, you have to like yourself. Those who show kindness usually have this down. So are you the kind of person that gives that nod or that unsolicited smile? If not, do a check in this area. You might be holding yourself from reaching out because you do not feel worthy of having anyone reach back.

Not Loving Your Potential

"I sit in a wheelchair all day."

"I can't ever play in that country club. I'm not the right color and I don't have enough money."

"I won't be able to play piano in front of that crowd because they expect better than I am."

All these negative voices we hear. My family would tell me day in and day out that I had the potential to be anything I wanted to be. Obviously, if I had wanted to be a professional basketball player for the Women's National Basketball Association I would have been justified in believing I would never get there. Okay. However, what about the fact I didn't love my true potential?

I knew I had book sense, could get along well with others, and enjoyed being a classroom. I had good times learning. However, I did not love the potential I knew I had to finish school or to be an executive or writer. I did not love that potential because I still did not believe I deserved it. I had not recognized God gave me that potential.

What I lacked to become a professional basketball player I made up for in ability to communicate and learn. However, I did not put everything into my studies until I embraced my potential. When I dropped out of school and was encouraged to return I depended upon others to embrace my potential.

One day my mind altered. It was clear God had given me these abilities and what I did with them was up to me. I could ignore them. I could talk myself out of the reality that the potential was there. However, I knew better. I knew the potential was there. I know the potential is there. I embrace it now. I move forward in my heart and mind day after day with the belief that my potential will both be developed and matured.

I learned to LOVE MYSELF.
I learned to ACCEPT MYSELF
I learned to LOVE MY POTENTIAL

All necessary to overcoming adversity. Remember what I said earlier that something like education does not prevent you from climbing upward. What prevents your climb is the mindset keeping you from getting that education. You are limited only by what you will not allow yourself to do.

Yes, it is true that in our world your skin color in many places might limit you. However, only at first. It is your duty to break through in order to get what you want. For decades, people of varied races and ethnicities had to break walls. If they did not break those walls, they would never have accomplished a thing. We have come far. Do not get me wrong. However, we still have to stand and break any wall that might get in our way. We cannot allow anything within our control to keep us down.

Sometimes when you have been called to have a relationship with God or you have been called to do things for God it might feel uncomfortable. My steps have been reordered. My steps have been reinforced since slipping into the coma.

The coma meant to me that my life was not only changing, but that my life could have ended. Suddenly things like getting what I wanted out of life were more important than anything. The fact that I had three strikes against me was irrelevant. My focus became on going after my life and defining it for myself. There would be nobody stopping me. This book is a result of choices I made to get where I have come.

Your relationship with God should be at the top of things you can control. A relationship with God is about making the choice to talk with Him, fellowship with Him, and trust in Him. Actions you take in life when in conjunction with trust in God can change everything.

Do not rip yourself off.
Learn to love yourself.

Learn to love your potential. First, you must believe in that potential.

One idea of getting support within your life is to find a group where women mentor women. There is nothing quite as liberating a group of women meeting in a home or coffee shop to share their fears, hopes, gripes, concerns, and joys. It can start small by just inviting women into your own home, or a nearby café. Invite a friend and have her invite someone you do not know, or do not know well. A group of five or six just visiting weekly or biweekly can give you great friendships and can eventually help change your life.

Nana was a praying parent. If you have kids, and perhaps those kids are part of the stress of your life, be a praying parent. You cannot always control the decisions your children might make, but you can turn them over to God. You can give God the freedom to run with your kids. If they are struggling in school, staying out too late, getting into trouble, or just seem to be unassociated with you, be a praying parent. What Nana did for me through prayer is incalculable. However, I will never doubt that she was right there for me as was God.

Find a mentor of your own. Look for people to surround yourself with. It is possible you just need someone to find in your life that inspires you to greatness because they are who you would like to become. Find out what they did to get there. If you can meet this person, perhaps talk with this person, that can only help. However, maybe this mentor is deceased or someone you are unable to meet. Read and find out all you can about them. Figure out how they achieved what they achieved. See what risks they made, and take risks. Listen to their philosophy and see if cannot apply to you.

In order to be walked on, you have to be lying down.
- Brian Weir

Strength of the Weak

God says the last will be first, the first will be last. What else do we need to know when we consider ourselves 'last'? What else do we need in our lives, especially when we feel we are as low as low can get? God promises we are first. He promises he is right there. We are the strong when we are the weak. Our weakness and humility lead to our strength.

Through the course work of UA, when you put these points into practice daily, you gain strength. You gain self-esteem, you gain self-worth, and you recognize the value of you. You become a stronger person. I dwell on this point because it is essential to becoming the person that you strive to become.

Have you ever met those people who walk around with an air of confidence, but you know better? Some people believe this false confidence is what God expects of them. Alternatively, they think society admires this confidence (and it does), but false is false. False confidence is fleeting. You can try to wear it, but it is thin. More than anything, you know it is false. No matter how long you try to wear it, it never becomes real.

Strength does not come by pretending to be someone we are not. This whole course is designed to create the you that is and always has been there. If we try to act in a way that is not genuine, we have not embraced the real us. Understand when I talk about confidence and being 'real,' I am not talking about acting. Acting will not get you anywhere. Moreover, you will have failed the course.

One of the keys to achieving greatness in the University of Adversity is to recognize and embrace your weaknesses. Through that recognition, you can gain real strength.

From Plantation to Platform

My ancestors, and perhaps yours, did not reach the stage where they had a voice by acting. Sure, there were times they had to act as if they believed they were subservient to white people. However, deep inside they knew better. They knew the weakness was in their color, not in their character. Once they embrace their equality, they pushed on society the fact that their color was not a weakness, but strength. Their voice came from turning their weakness into strength.

I had to do the same. I had to realize what made me weak in the eyes of society was actually the strength I needed to embrace.

It was an easy concept, but a difficult exercise. Once I began to embrace this strength, it was natural to move forward. I moved off my plantation and onto my platform.

- Write down what is true about you.
- What is your greatest weakness? If you could turn that your voice encourage others?
- Once you embrace this/these as a strength, how could your voice encourage others?
- Where would your message be most powerful?
- Do you feel you are acting in what confidence you show, or are you real? A mix?
- List three things you will do this week to try to embrace your weakness as a strength.
- List three things you will try to do in getting your message out.

Believers and Non-believers

Why is it that believers always find themselves stumbling and non-believers always seem to profit. Why does it not feel like God is on my side?

Have you ever wondered why it seems believers are struggling constantly? Week after week in church services, you hear prayer requests for sickness, weakness, financial woes, sin, family struggles, addiction, hurt. Is it because God tests us more than He tests non-believers? After all, it looks like non-believers are often more happy than believers.

Non-believers, many of them, seem to have no worries. They seem to be comfortable in their finances, their families appear happy, and they seem to have blessings. However, those blessings are not genuine. They are not blessings if they are not from God. Many are acting, many are unhappy inside, and many are in a great deal of denial.

Habakkuk was one of those servants that questioned the relevance of God. God seemed to be everywhere but paying a moments attention to Habakkuk. Nevertheless, he remained faithful. Habakkuk said, "God, I am going to wait right here and make myself available to you because I know you are going to speak to me and your words are going to be true." He trusted that even though God did not appear to be right there and attentive, His word was true. He trusted in that word. It proved to be the best and only choice Habakkuk had.

The Lord said write VISIONS- so that believers may be uplifted, so those who may hear it may continue the race. Make it plain if God said it, it is going to happen. So what do you want for your life? What is it that God can give you?

Dream big. Do not be afraid to ask if God wants to lift you up and take you above the clouds. Try it this minute. See how it makes you feel. See if God is not ready right now to change your mood or your life. You have dreams and no matter what your strikes you deserve those dreams. It is a matter of asking.

When you do not get those dreams answered, or those prayers answered, trust God, as we have talked about. However, do not give up on those dreams.

You have heard stories about people who overcame great obstacles. I am one of those stories. You can be as well. We want to add to the list of those who overcame great obstacles in the face of those who tried to tell us we could not. There is nothing more uplifting to God than when someone overcomes. Whether it is a people, an individual, a group, or a country… God rejoices when we overcome those things we are told we cannot overcome.

Keep away from people who try to belittle your ambitions. Small people always do that, but the really great make you feel that you, too, can become great.
- Mark Twain

What Are You Worried About?

God can only ask this question to those who have a relationship with him. What are you worried about? Do the bills pile up? Do you worry about your children? Their future?

We live in a society of great fear. With terrorism threats and wars raging around the world, we walk day in and day out in a great amount of fear. We walk under a colored bar code that could move at any moment upward and leave us in a fog of uncertainty. There is not a question of whether or not we are worried about something. The question is, is there ever a moment we are not worried?

When Jesus walked the earth, He said to his followers, "What are you worried about?" The reason this question only applies to believers is because the answer is, "If I have my eye on the sparrow, don't you think I'd watch out for you?" Only the believer can relate to the truth that God watches us even when it seems he is not around.

That is a leap of faith to let down our guard and trust in God. But can't we? Can we not trust that God is going to come through for us?

It might be the greatest test of all: can we leave it all up to God?

· Do you believe that God has His eye on you always?

· Do you believe God can be trusted in His word even when He does not seem to be right there?

· Do you believe you are protected as much as the sparrow is protected?

· List all the things you are worried about. Beside each, just write "God will take of this."

· Stop reading this book just long enough to think about whether you are really giving trust to God. Without this true trust in Him, you cannot make it through UA with complete thoroughness. You are only skimming by otherwise.

More than Meets the Eye

With God, you are more than appearance. Faith comes by hearing and hearing by the Word.

Is it not amazing to know, first, that we are more than our appearance? I know many believers and non-believers alike that this news should be the best news they have ever heard. How disgusted do you get watching television and seeing all these perfect faces, bodies, and voices? Do you know how many of those faces and bodies are not at all real? They are plastic! However, what is inside those plastic bodies? What is inside is what meets the eye, and that is the part you need to trust in.

There is not anything about you that is not pleasing to God if you trust in Him. This trust is demonstrated primarily through faith. Faith comes by hearing His word. Both by hearing and by reading. Constant contact with the Word will get you by in big ways. It is the secret to feeling that you have worth in this world no matter what you see in the mirror. What you should see is who and what is inside. A life full of faith is a life worthy of greatness.

For a moment try to see yourself as God sees you. Really, go from this world to a place beyond the clouds. Observe yourself sitting where you are, doing what you do. Do you think God is terribly concerned with anything other than what is inside? He is not. He sees your heart from way up there. He sees your deeds, and your deeds come from within. Your heart reflects your actions, and we are what we do... not what we look like.

We are more than meets the eye. We are more than what we see for ourselves.

Transient and Permanent

Problems of life, struggles of living is being able to discern the transient from the permanent. Some things are for now and some things are forever. Some things we pass through and some things we never escape. Some things are transient and some things are permanent. We value the transient and underrate the permanent. God is the giver of good things, but good things are not always permanent.

My speech reverted back to the deep, stressed sound as it was before the pump. We have to know what is transient from what is permanent. There are some things that need to last. We need to know what we have that one day we might lose. You tend to want to believe medical professionals, but they are human. When I had my surgery for my implant, I was told my muscles in my throat would relax and I would talk more clearly. I heard what the doctor said, but I was hoping that the impediment would not even be noticeable. My voice is still deep and that is just part of who I am.

Health and what we have cannot be taken away. A good sense of who I am, despite physical characteristics. The physical is transient, but who God made me is permanent. I am more than the three strikes. Both the Eternal and transient come from God, which is for life and which is forever. Some people think they are one and the same, but they are not. Life is within the physical life. Forever is beyond the physical life. Paul talks about those things that will fade away and those that will remain.

The Psalm (song) of love is Psalm 13.

Love is vital, eternal, and lasting.

Love is the only thing that will last and love is essential.

What you do is secondary to why you do it.

What is in your heart supersedes your actions. Attitude is more important than your performance. Everybody has a different gift, but they produce the same fruit. A gift is something you receive because God loves you. Fruit is what you produce because God loves you.

Our actions are often judged by those observing, when those are not the people that have the right to judge. The one that should judge is one receiving the fruit of our action. If I fix up a basket of food for a needy family and drop it off, an outside observer might think I am charitable or they might think I am a nosey person not minding my own business. Fact it, neither is necessarily true. I might just want the hungry to be fed.

Therefore, the only reliable judge is the one receiving food and God.

In fact, I cannot even judge myself. I can pretty much discount an impartial verdict there. If I start thinking too much, about how my actions are perceived, I will start watching my actions. Instead of feeding a hungry person, I will start worrying if I am giving them too much food, the wrong food, being snobby by giving lasagna instead of canned goods. It is not relevant. What is relevant is that I fed someone who was hungry.

Our actions matter only to the extent that we act out of love.

God gives out gifts to those that will use those gifts to produce fruit. It is not possible to produce fruit without receiving blessing. You can be saved and not have a gift. You cannot be saved and not produce fruit.

God says that faith without works is dead. This means we can be given salvation, we can be given gifts, but if we do not use those for good, if we do not use them for His glory, if we do not use our gifts to live up the holy name of God, then we have dead faith.

Dead faith is not the same as unsaved. You can be saved and have dead faith because you are not putting your faith to work. How does this apply to the UA? You cannot feel that you have overcome your issues without a genuine attempt at overcoming. You cannot overcome your strikes without some good works. It is through works that you have proven your reliance on faith, and you have shaken your dependence on those strikes. Our goal is to relive you of the pain and interference of the strikes.

Gifts come from an eternal God, but they are not guaranteed for an eternity. Love is not what you say, it is what you do. It is an action. Love is a behavior. At the end of this chapter, you will see the list of attributes of Love. Love is not just a behavior, but it is a lifestyle. Love is a noun and a verb. It is an action. Love is demonstrated through actions and through motive.

Earlier we said you could give things away and be charitable, but not have the faith to back it up. Its true faith without works is dead, but works without faith is equally dead. Works done through faith can change your life. They can change the lives of others. Works, actions, and charity through Love can change the world.

When one door closes, another opens. However, we often look so regretfully upon the closed door that we do not see the one that has opened for us.
- Alexander Graham Bell

The point for our purposes is there is no use for love and charity in UA without faith. Unless you have overcome (or are making great strides to overcome) your three strikes, you are not approaching these works without love. It is probable you are not even capable of making leaps in doing good deeds if you have not overcome those strikes.

- · How do you think your strikes prevent you from charity?
- · Do you do good deeds to show others you can, or do you do them through love?
- · List two things you can do this week to show love, but do them so that nobody notices.
- · When you complete those two things, write how you felt. Did you do them because I said so? Can you put this into practice at least once or twice in your life on a weekly basis?

Like so much of life, actions are a result of habit. Practice makes perfect.

Paul writes that love without action is cheap. We talk of moments in our lives where we have the best of intentions, but we never follow through with those intentions. To use a cliché we say, "The road to hell is paved with good intentions."

How sad would it be to find ourselves at the end of the day (our lives) standing before God with a whole list of things we wish we had done? God's reply might very well be, "Why didn't you do them?"

"Well, God, it sounds crazy now, but I didn't think I could pull them off."

"Why?"

"I'm black. I am handicapped. I'm a woman."

"And?"

"Well, they told me I couldn't do those things I wanted to do because of who I am."

"And didn't you hear when I said that through me you can do all things?"

"I did. I'm sorry."

Overcome those strikes, friend. Do not let this day end without working through this UA course and trying to change the lives of those around you.

Gifts are useless without love. Giving without love is just a ceremony.

The Effects of Love

1) Love builds up, love is patient. Paul realized people are more weak than wicked. Love believes in possibilities. More to me than meets the eye. Love does not desert me. When I fall, after I fall in love, God believes I can go higher than before the fall.

2) Christ-like love has an heir of graciousness. Real love cares more about what it can give than what it can take.

3) People who know how to love know how to give.

4) Love does not keep a bank account on what others do.

5) Love gives us power to endure all things.

6) Love is essential, effectual, and eternal.

7) Faith is good, Hope is grand, but Love is better.

God is not faith, but I have faith in Him
God is not hope, though all my hope is based on Him.
God is Love; whoever abides in Him abides in Love

This love is not simply directed toward God. You have to show it towards humanity. Love that forgives and strives to forget.

Chapter Seven

Do You Know Who You Are?

Second Best

How many times have you seen a World Series second place team praised? Our society does not celebrate those that come in second place. We are only interested in the winner. We are too focused on the on the number one position, but we should not forget about number two. After all, why should we not? God will help you discover who you are. Be happy with who you are.

What are the odds that you will come out as number one in whatever field you are working? How are those things measured anyway? It should be enough that we try as hard as we can. If we come in second, how amazing is that? Should we not celebrate when we succeed on any level?

In Leah's world she was impaired, cross-eyed. She tried to be herself and discover her uniqueness. To the contrary, most of the world is beautiful and balanced. However, Leah eventually did not care. She thrived as who she was. We are told Paul was not the brightest bulb in the world or easy on the eye. How many people do you know, believers or non-believers, that can tell you who Paul was? Almost everyone. He sure did not let his strikes get in the way. If you cannot appreciate what I have done to overcome my strikes, look at Paul. He was the ultimate man with strikes and overcame them. He might have ended second in his world, but in God's world, Paul ran the race as a good and faithful servant.

Regulated contests push toward one goal. Honest competition creates an environment where everybody wants to win, wants to wear the victor's crown. # 1 gets the gold. #2 gets the silver. Those Olympic sports can sometimes get silly. The separate number one from number two by nanoseconds. Two nanoseconds! How absurd is it when we beat ourselves up over nanoseconds when what we have done to get there is an amazing feat?

· Who are you in God's eye?
· Who are you in your own eye?
· Are you first, second or only a runner in a race where the end has rewards plentiful for all that stay the course?

Nothing is as strong as gentleness, and nothing is as gentle as true strength. - *St. Francis De Sales*

Individualism

Rigorous sense of Individualism abides within our culture. Everyone is concerned about winning, being at the top, being noticed as the best. However, we forget about number two. Isaiah said God's ways are not our ways and His thoughts are not his thoughts. In order to come to terms with God, we need to look at the world the way God wants us to. We have to turn away from the world's thoughts and develop our own.

When I was in school, I could not afford to think of the world in the same way it sees itself. For one, I could not think of myself the way I was seen. I could not allow myself to put myself in the box the world wanted to put me in. I became an individual in my own mind, and that individualism defined who I was. I was not defined by just my strikes or as that "special" girl. I became Diedra the individual. I was only what I thought of myself.

We are all individuals and all number one based on who we need to be. God created us in His image. We have an obligation not only to be the individuals God made us, but we must live that person inside and out to the world around us. It is vital we embrace our individuality in order for God to use us.

God always took the same three men when something significant was about to happen. He chose these three men because of who they were, and because they had embraced themselves as individuals.

Peter- Impetuous, always talking before thinking.

James- Egotist.

John- Egotist.

Andrew was the exception. He rarely made the spotlight as he was an ordinary man. He was concerned about the King's business. Andrew did not embrace his individuality or even who

God wanted him to be. He wanted to stay where it was comfortable. Andrew remained loyal where loyalty was rewarded in the here and now. There is nothing wrong with this type of individuality, but we risk missing becoming who God wants us to be.

The majority of the world, the nation, is comprised of Leah's not Rachel's. There are more Leahs then Rachel's living in society. People with impediments. Anything that represents impairment contrary to what we call a beautiful or balanced personality. These people are relegated to the status of inferiority. It's was up to Leah to make it clear she would not accept the inferiority complex. She would not accept it, nor should you. You cannot.

Leah did not try to be anybody but Leah. She was not into finding the spotlight. Not only was she okay with number two, or more, Leah had reached a point where she accepted the steps in the last chapter. She accepted her place, she loved herself, she liked herself, and she was excited about her potential future because she knew God was in charge. She started a pilgrimage of discovering her own uniqueness. God will help you discover your grand place. Once this is revealed you can then discover who you are. Be happy with who you are.

I imagine a world where the idea of being inferior does not exist. It is a world where people do not think of lesser-than. There would be no lesser-than. It is a world far from where we are, and I do not think it begins anywhere but within those of us that have these lesser-than opinions of ourselves. Because once we start acting otherwise, others will not be able to force their views on us. When we make the lesser-than mentality obsolete within ourselves, it will disappear in the world.

This course at UA helps, I believe, to remove that stigma. Once you see yourself as God sees you, then you cannot ever see yourself less than this again. It is not possible. This is another of our goals, then, in our time together, help alleviate and accept your three strikes and to never think of yourself as inferior again. Once you overcome that inferiority, you will start to live a life undreamt.

Trust in yourself for this. Trust in God for this. Be faithful to what God expects of you, how He wants you to see yourself, as He sees you, and trust that life will turn out in your favor. Once you have truly embraced this, God will reward you.

God said, "If you are faithful in a few things, I will make you ruler over many."

When You Are the Last Choice

The world looks at the external. As adolescents, we may get over the feeling of being the last choice, but as adults, we enter different arenas of the overlooked and the ignored. It can be as general as standing in line at the grocery store and being passed by someone that disrespects you, all the way to constantly being passed up for job promotions. Many reasons exist as to why adults might enter back into this "last choice" situation.

I was never the one on the sports teams chosen to pitch, throw the dodge ball, or even serve as a sideline cheerleader. Of course, I had no desire to be one of the main cheerleaders, but the point is I could not have served in any capacity whatever. Not for lack of want or ability, but because I was usually the last choice.

- When was the last time you were chosen 'last' or overlooked unfairly?
- How did you feel? What did you do?
- Have you ever treated someone as 'last' or passed them up when you knew better?
- Think of your spouse or children or a family member you think might be 'passed up' for something they wanted and deserved. How did you help them overcome their disappointment?

God does not want us to think of ourselves in the same terms others think of us. He wants us to overcome those feelings of being inferior to others. The UA is all about changing your mindset and finding what it is about you that needs to change in order to becoming what you want to become. Your dreams are within your reach, but it requires your overcoming your strikes.

When you are people's last choice, you might be God's first choice.

God will position you where He wants you when you are ready. You will be positioned via an anointing. The anointing makes the difference. What do I talk about when I talk about the anointing?

Anoint Divine communication of the gifts are necessary for the position. God will put you in a position to make great change, and you will be given the gifts to fulfill that position. God puts in me the gifts necessary for the position. Anointing divine infiltration of the power. The anointing is a direct divine intervention where God touches you through His Spirit and you are changed. Anointing by pouring of the oil, symbolizes God coming into your life. When you believe you have been given a calling, or a Pastor has anointed you with oils, or God touches you.

You might think you do not need an additional anointing to be given the gifts of the Spirit. You might feel you already have the gifts imbedded in your personality. Moreover, you might be correct that you are very gifted. However, once you are given a command from God to take responsibility in a new position, God touches you and you will need an anointing. Even King David needed an anointing.

The reason David needed the anointing means he was lacking something naturally. The anointing compensates for what you are lacking naturally. The anointing from God comes via the Holy Spirit. It is a request you make, or something that overcomes you once you have opened yourself to the blessings of God.

The Holy Ghost will do one of two things.

1) He will put something in you that you naturally do not have, or

2) He will release through you that what you already had that what would have never been manifested if it was not hooked up to the power.

You will change the world around you in ways you cannot imagine. It is an additional gift for believers. Without the anointing, you can make change, without question. However, you might not be making the change that God requests of you. You will get this when you have yet to have the possibility for significant impact.

Sit down before fact as a little child. Be prepared to give up every preconceived notion, follow humbly wherever and whatever abysses nature leads, or you will learn nothing.
* - Thomas H. Huxley*

Starting With Me

Forget about first, second, or any placing. God is not interested in your placing. As we have mentioned, He said the first should be last anyway, so forget about the placing. Think about God simply starting with you. Inside you, just a simple desire to be what He wants you to be. Nothing more and nothing less. Only what God wants for you.

God's favor in His power, His person, His blessings, and all that He has aimed in your direction. God's favor puts you in spots that you ordinarily would not be in if it were not for His favor, His choice. God's favor is that point in life when He puts you where other people have tried to prevent you from getting to. People, sin, bad experiences; all have the potential to stop you from where God wants you to be. His favor exalts you.

Let us discuss this for a moment. Keep in mind we are not interested in turning the graduates of UA into their own little church. We are concerned with turning ourselves into what we can potentially become. We want to become who God meant for us to become. It is not enough just to go to church. It is not really even a requirement to attend a church. This is a relationship with God, and a new direction for your life, and for my life. It is about changing who we are, not about putting ourselves into a situation that is not who we are.

Sin keeps us from God, but at the same time, sin is inevitable in our world. We will all sin. If do not there is not any reason for a savior. If we could keep ourselves from sinning, Jesus would be irrelevant. Therefore, we cannot expect to become perfect. UA is not about making you a better Christian, or even about making you a Christian. UA wants to make you a better person, to show that society cannot keep you down, to lift you beyond your day to day.

Remember one of the steps in the UA is to keep blame placed in the right direction. Do not blame others for your issues; they have their own baggage anyway. To resolve your own issues, you have to start with you. Some things you have to cleave and some things you have to leave. Part of gaining the individuality we talked about earlier is leaving behind the old you, and cleaving to the individual you are.

It is tough to discover who God wants you to be. Part of the discovery process is tearing away, or isolating, those things you need to peel away. Another part of the process then is to cleave to those items you decide are you.

- What do you need to relieve yourself of?
- How can you get rid of these things keeping you from being yourself? How can God help?
- How would you like the world to see you?
- What traits do you have that enhance that image?
- List the ways that today you can begin to leave what needs leaving, and cleave those things you must cleave to.

When I was at Matheny School, God tried to start with me. On Sunday mornings, I used to hide in the bathroom to get out of chapel. You cannot hide from God whether you stay home or hunker in a chapel bathroom. God is everywhere and hiding is useless. That is not our point in this exercise.

A month before my overdose I met a man named Bob while I was shopping. He carried my bags to the car and told me he believed in Angels. He said he saw five of them around me. When I woke up from my coma, I remembered that conversation and I was certain one of those Angels was my Nana Cole. You probably have angels around you as well. Embrace those angels. Let them protect you.

Joshua said choose you this day who you will serve. Nevertheless, God chooses His children. God chose me in spite of my rebellion and immaturity. When God has singled you out you will get to where He wants you to be in spite of yourself, roadblocks, or any fear. God's agenda supersedes even the one you have for yourself.

What people think are the strikes against you are the very reasons God uses you.

More Than What You See

When we talk of God using you in first, second, or third place, we think about running a race. However, we only need to finish this race; we do not have to win. That means when you wake up in the morning and you are heading out to your day, you do not have to struggle to win. You just have to finish and in that finishing you have won. No matter the position you finish in.

What a relief. What a good God we have. So what if you ever become convinced that you cannot finish the race, that the run is just too much? What would cause you to feel this way? That is right, now you are catching on. Your strikes. Everything you feel keeps you from finishing the race, from loving your potential, is absolutely a strike. Usually many little "strikes" can be whittled down to a few major strikes. However, we are more than what we see. Oh, so much more.

The message that we preach, or speak, or write is bigger than the messenger. Yet, God entrusts us to this message.

Another cliché…do not judge a book by its cover. That is a life lesson as well. Do not judge a person by their looks. Not only the negative looks but the positive as well. You might see a good-looking Hollywood type and figure that person has it all together. Do not bet on it. In fact, they might have more strikes than even they might know.

What you see may not be what you get.
What you see may not be the whole story.

Be careful judging people on what you see. We are more than our looks, our titles, our money, what we lack, what we own. Inside we are bigger than all those things. If we judge based on superficial things we will miss what is important about people. We will miss the things that give us the most joy. How many people do you meet and are impressed by what they do and the whole conversation winds up having only discussed their external elements and not their internal. You still do not know who they are. You missed it. You missed the whole point of meeting another human. You missed the joy of what God gives us. Even more, they missed knowing you. It was a lost opportunity.

We limit ourselves by what society says we are. We are who we are.

Let God reveal the mystery of what you will be.
Let God reveal the certainty of who you will be.

Lord of the Left-Handed

Faith comes by hearing and hearing comes through the Word. There is no other way to come by faith than to understand the message of the Lord and the messenger of the Lord's Word. There are more outlets than ever today to hear the Word. You can get it on radio, on television, at every church corner, in books, in some newspapers, and in private schools. There is no excuse these days not to get access to the Word. Just like 'Word

Up,' the slang we talk about, is the Word of God that is up. Word Up!

As a Christian, it is difficult to accept my own imperfection. One of the reasons is that God is the God of healing. If He wanted, I know without question He could heal me. He could reach right into my body and change the way my muscles function, the way my mind works, the way I live day to day. He could do it. So, why not?

This goes to our discussion on unanswered prayers. There is a reason, and I have to trust in that reason. Seek the best to give to God. Sometimes you wish your inabilities could be abilities. I know if God wanted me to run the marathon in His glory, I would. So why does he not take a person with my heart and my intent and create someone that is not perceived to be stricken with three strikes?

Enod was not able to use his right hand. The strength of Enod's left hand emphasized the weakness of his right. Our handicaps speak louder than our abilities. Inabilities get center stage and your abilities get back stage. People tend not to introduce you by your name but by rumor or title or "So and so is a lawyer." When someone that is handicapped is introduced it is usually by stating, "This is the daughter of so and so." It is rarely, "This is Sarah who graduated from University of Chicago."

We have much to overcome in this life, and it is not possible to do it under the old ways of thinking. It takes new thinking. It takes new thinking on our part. You have to look at yourself in a different light, and others will see you the same.

The difference between a Saint and a Sinner is when a Saint falls they get back up. We have to get back up both literally and figuratively. It is not easy walking when you are handicapped physically. It is not easy walking spiritually when you are handicapped in your thinking. You must think like a Saint, act like a Saint, read like a Saint, and when you fall, you get back up like a Saint. We are all going to fall sometimes.

Do to cerebral palsy, my walking is unsteady. When I used to fall, I used to curse and get back up. I asked God to take away the profanity. Now when I fall I just get back up.

One day at work, I was tired so I got on the floor to file. I figured if I changed my position, I would feel better. When I got on the floor and continued my task I still felt physically tired, but I kept on saying to myself, "Mind over body." I reached my goal for that day. All those files were put away. I reached my goal. Did I make a huge dent in the world? Maybe not. However, it was a huge success for me because I could have stopped. I could have gone home, or rested, but the task was completed because I kept going even when I felt as if I could not do another thing.

Chapter Eight

Faith for Tough Times

Is faith an empty virtue? Is the idea of believing in something you cannot see more than you are ready to commit to? After all, faith is believing in something you cannot prove. There is no science to faith. But what you do have in faith is miracle. Again, not something you can "prove," but an experience. In fact, it is more real than some science. Give me medicines and tell me they cure my headache or backache and the best I can do is trust you. However, watch a woman's life change and have her praise God for it, and you know. You know.

A Father interceded on his sick daughter's behalf. Mystics call it the dark night of the soul—Tough Times. In the midst of tough times, hold on to your faith. Your faith will sustain you.

Faith comes in times of trouble and in need. You have faith that life will develop for you as you want it to develop. After all, we are asking you to believe that those strikes holding you down for most of your life can be lifted from you and no longer be a burden. I am making that promise to you and that is a promise I make in faith. However, you have to accept that faith in order for UA to work for you.

What kind of faith did the father have?

1) Confrontational—do not let your title get in the way of you interacting with Jesus. While you were in the process of becoming. (Do not forget once you become.) Nana interceded on my behalf when I could not.

2) Confident – Do not give up on the situation too soon. The father kept making the situation known. He kept praying until he blessed him. I am going to be like Jacob and wrestle until you bless me. Sometimes we pray prayers with no expectations.

3) Challenged – No matter how strong your faith is it will be challenged. Divine delays do not mean divine denials.

What do you do in tough times when you hear that negative voice?

1) Ignore the voice.

2) Hear His Word – The very thing that God requires from you he will give it to you. God will send you a word which will contradict your reality HIS word says fear not only believe.

3) Stay on the course of your journey.

We all have our negative voices. We all have those times when we not only hear them, but we believe them. We can sit for hours on end in our kitchen, on our porch, or in a hospital room and know without doubt life will not get better. We might believe this to the point it makes us weep. We cry. We want to end our lives, perhaps, because of nothing but negative voices.

Can you control those voices?

Not only can you control those voices, but you can absolutely make them go away. You can make those voices positive. You can change them and everything they do to you. Not only can you, but you must. It is vital that you get those voices under control.

Great changes may not happen right away, but with effort, even the difficult may become easy.

- Bill Blackman

Take all the advice poured out in this book and commit it to your soul. We strive to rise above where we are. Everyday humans in countries worldwide want to be better. They want to gain more whether in love or in respect. Life is a challenge for the healthiest and for the wealthiest. Everyone has their struggles. Everyone has their strikes.

Our goal should not be to become rich, but rather that potential richness comes out of our goal of bettering ourselves. We all want respect, but respect is not our final goal. It is by being true to ourselves that we gain respect. We must to be who we are.

In a time not all that long ago, African-American people wanted only to be recognized as equal as they were equal in God's eyes. Women wanted equality because they were equal in God's eye. Today, debates rage over "alternate" lifestyles, but what lifestyle hasn't always been alternate at one time? Slavery and women's "place" was always ignorantly fought by incorrect use of scripture. We must not use the Word to discriminate, but rather to lift one another up. Discrimination is when we allow our "strikes" in the eyes of society to get us down.

We go down, we let them kick us, and we do not fight. We should fight. We should fight the good fight left to us from before, and the harder we fight now the less our children will have to fight.

I see the UA course as liberation for all that seek societal change. It has been said before, and will be said again. You can change the world one person at a time. Begin with yourself, then you will love others, then the world will be a new and vibrant place. I believe there is no perfection this side of Heaven, but I believe people should not live in such a way it is impossible to gain respect because of something out of our control.

Our strikes, whether color, handicap, economic, or health, should not be our downfall. God gave us these afflictions for us to grow. Or rather, He allowed these afflictions. I do not believe God purposefully gives us struggle. Struggle is a result of evil. It is a result of sin from the day Adam and Eve made the wrong decisions for their lives. At that point, God allowed a portion of our lives to be ruled by sin. This is our curse.

God does not force us to suffer. However, through sin, we sometimes must suffer and use what we learn and gain for the glory of God. By overcoming, we prove our worth. The day slavery ended is the day a people were liberated to become who God meant for them to become. Streets are riddled with violence, drugs, and death. Education suffers to this day for African-American children. We expect our government to intervene, but it should be evident this will never happen. Not necessarily because our government does not care, but because it cannot.

We need to overcome our own personal strikes, and then little by little reveal, expose, and eliminate the strikes without our own government. UA is a step toward a huge goal not for individuals only, but for a nation. Eventually for a world.

This is Diedra's dream. This is the spirit my Nana embedded in me. However, I realize it is one person at a time. It is one woman, one African-American, one handicapped fighter at a time that that stands and lifts praise and prayer to God, hoping against all odds of society that someday we will prevail.

That is why I wrote this book, why I decided to tell my story. I know it is something that can change the world if we only start with ourselves first. If we sit down and take a hard look at our lives, we will recognize where we need to make changes. We know we are not all we should become for God. We are living on the sidelines, we are hoping for change to be given to us. My family and my church taught me that only from within myself can real change come. So I wrote this, letting you know as well.

By now, you should have come to many new conclusions about your life. If you have answered the questions I pose throughout, you should have lists upon lists of how you can change your life and the lives of those around you. If you do not have those lists, go back. Do yourself a favor and return to those questions asking them, and answering them honestly. In order to graduate from UA, you must learn honesty to yourself. There is no point reaching the end of this book without having asked those hard questions.

If you do not want to ask them, is it because you are involved in a battle with yourself? Is there a battle raging with yourself? Perhaps a battle between good and evil. A battle of will versus spirit? Our personal will often trumps our spiritual will. God gave us the ability to make choices. He gave us free will. Our spirits cause us to yearn for something bigger; we yearn for the things of God. But they do not come easy, and our will sometimes chooses to say no to what our spirit yearns.

Spiritual Warfare vs. Physical Combat

Wisdom is gained by going through a spiritual warfare. God is a God of battle and since that day Satan was allowed to infiltrate Earth, we became a battleground between right and wrong. Between will and spirit. We war amongst nations, but we war in a spiritual sense even more. In fact, I would argue that many of our earthy wars are fought because of spiritual defects. We must discern between the things of the world and things of God.

Discern

1. To perceive with the eyes or intellect; detect
2. To recognize or comprehend mentally

The earthly army vs. God's army is motivated to war for very different reasons. The earthly armies claim to fight for land, freedom, liberty, money, or sometimes nothing more than claim to victory. Spiritual warfare is quite different.

Spiritual warfare is of the soul. Since time began, God could stake claim to His creation, but Satan wanted to intervene and betray God. Therefore, Satan tries to claim those souls that belonged to God in the first place. It is not about land or property or money with God, though Satan will sometimes make you think it is. It is about your soul.

When you are feeling down or depressed, Satan can begin claiming a victory. However, God wants that victory and He wants you to overcome. He will, in the end, win the fight. Jesus on the cross won that fight for us. It remains a struggle, however, day in and day out, to just believe God is on our side.

Imagine the fight in days of slavery when a white landowner could tell another man he was no better than the pigs. In fact, some fattened pigs had more worth than a female, handicapped woman. We know that is not right. We know that is sin. However, it was the state of affairs.

Imagine in those conditions the state of the souls of those men and women abused because of their skin color. However, we had the spiritual battle on our side. We had a God of love on our side. A God that told us, deep in our souls, we are His people with more worth than even the angels. My people believed this and it kept them fighting. Those spirituals were sung from places so deep in the soul.

You ever been to an all black church? Did you ever notice how the services tend to get lively or how the walls can sometimes shake? It is because that Word has always been what pulled our people through. The same jubilation our ancestors needed just to survive a day is that same jubilation we feel today when we want to stand and tell the world how great our God is. I am a fighter in the spiritual war.

The earthly army would not accept me because I was not physically fit to fight in war, but you do not have to be physically fit for God's army. You do not have to be physically fit for the gift of discernment. God just needs your heart, He needs your commitment, and He needs your soul. He needs you to offer yourself to Him to be used in big ways.

Our earthly army wants your body. They can entice you with all kind of goodies in return for your time, your life, your physical strength, perhaps your physical life. They want dedication without question. They want blind faith that their mission is the right mission, and that you will not question it. How many people do we know that get in trouble for questioning their mission during wartime? It is not acceptable in the earthly army. Yet God allows you question what you need to question. There is no problem in His eyes because His will is perfect and His motive is of Heaven.

UA is a school of the spirit that you can choose to enter or ignore. Our will battles with our Spirit because the easy road seems filled with a smooth path. However, believe me, all roads on this Earth have bumps. Do not choose the road without God because you think it is easier. The road with or without God is rough, so why not have the Creator walking with you? Once you enter UA full throttle, once you ask the tough questions, one you let God in, and most of all once you accept your three strikes as potential strengths, you will have become a honor roll student. You will have moved to a place of peace as I did, and out of the pit of despair.

The Army is a place for physical war. A place where your choices are rather closed. You cannot make choices in the Army. They are made for you. You do not get to choose your meal, where you sleep, where you serve, or these days you do not even get to choose when you leave. Our country has us to embattle in wars abroad that retired military are called back. It is a physical war with limited choices. God's army, and you join in once you come into UA, is full of choices. However, best of all, the retirement package includes Heaven, and it can never be recalled.

What are the determining factors in choosing to enlist in the army rather than enrolling in a school?

1) Money

School costs a lot these days, and the army will pay the way. But the UA is free. God already paid the way into His Spiritual Army.

2) Opportunities

Your opportunities are limited in the physical army. You might even think you are done and then be called back in, pulled from your life and family into a war you did not start. God has unlimited opportunities, and He will guide you on the right path every time.

3) Goals/Direction for life

The army decides your life. It takes you from your family, it puts you in a country of its choice, and you serve until it says you are done. God will take you where you will be safe, guided, and your Spirit filled.

4) Travel

Travel in the army is guaranteed, though you do not know how many bombs will go off in your bunker day after day. Your travel with God is guaranteed too. On the Last Day, you travel with Him to see those that have gone before, resting in the arms of the Savior forever.

5) Convenience

The Earthly army is full of monetary rewards, but your life becomes the military. In God's army, you live your life for Him, and you will forever be in His sight. Your life belongs to Him, but as the Creator, there was never any escaping Him anyway.

The University of Adversity's Motto is: *We are designed to strengthen your life in spite of your adversity.*

This University is mobile. You can take it with you. The military offers travel. No matter where you find yourself you can take your learning with you. In addition to the University being mobile, there is another claim to fame. This University can lay claim to being the oldest universal unfounded institution. For ages, since Biblical times, we have had to learn to overcome our adversity.

Adversity in your life as a result of your strikes can be overcome by study in the University, anytime, anywhere. God has given us this ability, through his wisdom, to recognize and overcome our strikes. Even as you have gone through this book, you have been taking classes on various themes and courses necessary to complete the tasks. The questions have been tough, sometimes, but necessary to drive home the points you must recognize to 'be all you can be.'

There are no written exams to enroll at the UofA. No SATs or ACTs. You cannot SAT, you must ACT, but you do not have to pass any written exams. The final exam is at the end of the path, when you have overcome you adversities. You will need to receive the learned information by one or all of these entrances. It depends on your disposition (or how you ACT) in order to advance within UofA.

The three entrances are:

1. Physical Entrances – See, Hear, Touch

a. It is possible you might even have limitations here. Perhaps this is one of your personal strikes. You will learn to see, hear, and touch God in ways you never dreamed. Even if you are blind, deaf, or impaired in arms and legs you will still touch God. Moreover, God will touch you. Believe in this and you have passed entrance number one.

2. Physiological Entrances – Mind, Body, Soul

a. Your mind will tune in to God and his Word. You will be readied to learn His word, and be open to when he speaks to you.

b. Your body, even if part of your strike, will be given to God. You have the promise of healing anytime between now and that Last Day. Once you give your body to God, the Holy Temple that stores our Soul, God will bless you.

c. Your soul, once you turn your life over to God, becomes His and is His eternally. This Earth is just a passing phase for our Soul. It is here the decision is made as to where our Soul spends eternity. Coming into the UA gives your Soul a ticket to Heaven.

3. Spiritual Entrances – Father, Son, Holy Ghost

a. Once you see, hear, and touch God you move into a new spiritual dimension.

b. Once you give your mind, body, and soul to God, even with their imperfections, you enter into a relationship with the Holy Trinity. You become aware of the Father (God), the Son (Jesus), and the Holy Ghost. The Holy Ghost lives inside you, and will drive you closer to God day after day as you walk with Him.

One of those physiological entrances, the soul, is defined as the spiritual part of our bodies. It is our connection to God. The soul is what was before our physical bodies were born, and what we have once our physical bodies have moved on. Our outside is important to maintain in terms of being able to perform the duties God has asked us to perform. However, our soul must be maintained forever.

Soul

· The animating and vital principle in humans credited with the faculties of thought, action, and emotion and often conceived as an immaterial entity.

· The spiritual nature of humans, regarded as immortal, separable from the body at death, and susceptible to happiness or misery in a future state.

· The disembodied spirit of a dead human.

There is a list of learned or instilled traits that will help you excel at the University. Once you begin to demonstrate the traits below, you will be well on your way to success within the UA. Remember, the UA never actually ends. It is a lifelong learning process. So if you cannot pick up all the traits below quickly, be patient. Pray for them, and God will make you aware of them in time.

Discipline
Faith
Love
Hope
Compassion
Discretion

When the Odds Are Against You

A mass of people gathered as they were hungry, perhaps near starved. Thousands of people. Five thousand or more. In addition, their food supply consisted of five loaves of bread and two fish. You can imagine the grumblings.

"We're going to die."

"Who planned this anyway?"

"Should we start gathering more? Should we complain? Should we...what should we do?"

Jesus was standing by and because there was unlimited demand and a limited supply, He was not bothered. By the end of the gathering, everyone was filled. These people did not have all the traits to pass the tests of UA. However, you must learn or develop those traits. The above example shows how Jesus demonstrated patience to these people, and that same patience is showed to you. You must practice faith that He has it under control.

Because of the three strikes against us, the odds of success are limited, though our desire is unlimited. These odds might retard our progress in society, but with the unlimited power and love of God, we have nothing to fear or worry about. Moreover, if you take on the attributes of that individual you want to become, the one that God means for you to become, you will not have any fears. You will overcome those strikes. You will reclaim your life.

In gambling, the odds are you will not make more than you spend. You might win some of the time, but over time, you will lose more than you put in. There is not a guaranteed means of winning in a casino, at the racetrack, at the poker table. However, with God you are the House and the odds are always in your favor. You might not win all of the time, but you will win more times than not. At the end of the game, you stand the victor.

In this world, the odds are never against us. Not in God-terms. Nevertheless, it might seem that they are. In fact, the idea of three strikes is that 'you're out.' Once you are out, you are supposed to not be able to play the game anymore. Therefore, these three strikes make us think we are completely out of the game. At least the odds are so stacked against us we are out of luck. We cannot let our internal fears keep us down. We cannot let how the world perceives us influence how we perceive ourselves. What do you do when the odds are against you? What do you do when you look around and feel you are completely alone, and that nothing you ever do will matter?

You might be tempted to wave the flag of surrender. There is no magical solution. However, here are some things to consider.

1) Recognize what you have, start where you are, use what you have, do what you can. The temptation is to be intimidated

with what you do not have. Many times, when trying to solve a problem, we leave our own resources.

2) Make plans to eat even when there is no physical sign that things are going to come through. Structure your situation for the blessing. Be still and let God control the situation. Prepare yourself for the blessing even before you receive it. Do it God's way. Corporations may cheat, scheme, become unethical. You might have a cushy job one day and the next the CEO pulls it out from under you. It happens every day. That CEO does not stop eating, but you fear you might. God never pulls out the rug. He never blind sides us. Trust in that.

3) Take your trouble and transfer ownership. Do you believe that God asked us to lay our burdens at His feet? Because He did, and he not only asks it, He demands it. Lay your burdens, your strikes, at His feet and let Him deal with them.

4) Thankfulness. Thank God for what you do have. Temptation is to be cynical or critical. Or even worse, we tend to only look to God when things are bad. However, when life is good all around you, turn to God and thank Him for the blessings. Always look on the bright side of life. Never allow your cynical feeling run your day-to-day choices and attitude.

5) Stewardship- Is what you do after the blessing. What you do after the blessing is what determines if the odds are going to be against you in the next situation. Once you make it, you have to do the right thing with what you got. You have to give back to those around you when you have been given something. That is not to say if you make a large sum of money that you need to give it away. That money might be there to help you. However, it does mean you must meet needs you see around you. Maybe a neighbor has trouble getting downtown to shop. Do your part to see they have a way. Be a good steward with what God gives you, and you will always have more than you need.

To reach a port we must sail, sometimes with the wind and sometimes against it. However, we must not drift or lie at anchor.

- Oliver Wendell Holmes

Situations Beyond Your Control

Every time you think you have the answers to life's questions, they change the question. Life has the element of the unexpected. You never know what to expect from one moment to another. What were we all planning for September 12, 2001?

Didn't matter did it? After that heinous terrorist attack all of our lives changed. Our plans were cancelled. Our lives were altered and changed. We did not prepare for it, we could not prepare for it, but it was forced upon us.

People lost their families, husbands, and wives in the attack. Who can plan for that? You do not know the future. Whenever you error and cannot find the eraser, whenever you faltered and failed and people do not want to forgive, you are in a situation beyond your control. God specializes in the impossible. There is nothing we can do that God will not forgive once we ask Him for that forgiveness. It is quite impossible, however, to get all those around us to forgive us. No matter what we do, it seems when we need to be forgiven, few people are there for it to happen. However, that never happens as far as God is concerned. Never. God's timing is never wrong, either.

Whenever Jesus wants to meet your situation, you have to be at the right place and the right time. You could miss your blessing. This is a prerequisite for receiving a blessing. When they say Jesus shows Himself to us when we least expect it, you better believe it. Keep yourself alert and aware at all times. When you need a blessing (when you need more fish than you have on hand) wait for God. He will come on His time, and you will be blessed.

However, it is also possible for the blessing to come when you are not ready, and that is not something you want to miss out on. Can it be possible to know that you missed a blessing?

When your life is out of contact with God, assume you are missing blessings all around. You may never know otherwise, but you should assume it. Especially if you are in a rut and need God's blessing. If you are not on His side at the moment, you will not get that blessing. Do you want to be made whole?

There was a man whom God was ready to bestow a blessing upon. The man had several strikes against him, and he made several bad choices.

1) Preoccupied with the problem—cannot find a solution. The man thought only of the problem, and did not look for a solution.

2) Blaming others for the condition.

He thought everyone else must be to blame, and he did not think to consider how he might be able to change his mind or his situation.

3) Too busy complaining about what he did not have and could not see what he had. As it turns out, his situation was not that bad. He had more around him than he dreamed, but his cynical nature caused him to look only at the negative. He did not stop to count his blessings.

4) Waiting for Angels when he had Jesus. He wanted more. He wanted proof. He was not his life to be something other than what it was. He did not trust God, he trusted only in things he could not have.

Solution

1) This man was challenged to take Jesus at his word. Take Jesus at His word. It is okay to challenge Him, but trust in the answer that you are given.

2) Forget about what you think might happen and take me at my word.

Do not write the plan yourself. Let God write the plan.

3) Rise up and take your bed. When it is time to move, move. Trust God. Even though you are comfortable in your bed, warm, safe and perhaps even content...trust God. Take Jesus at His word.

4) Display your deliverance. Show others your new attitude. Display to those around how God changed your life and your attitude. Show how he has delivered you.

Chapter Nine

Blessings of Being Kept

There is no challenge trusting in God in the midst of good times. The challenge is trusting in God when your foundation is not stable or has been taken away. Is there still joy when I am sick, when I am lonely, when I lost my popularity, when I have been ostracized and criticized? Is there still joy?

There is not joy at that moment, and God understands that we are going to experience hurt. However, once that hurt passes, once we have gained our composure, we should not dwell there. We have to trust that God did not want us to go through what Satan put in our path, but if we turn our trust back to God, he will deliver us from that bump in the road.

How can one come to God if they come only during good times? It is when we are in the midst of adversity that we believe God has left us alone. This is the true test. This is when you have to say, "God is good. God is there. God is all around." It is the truest test of all when coming through UA.

My name, in its many variations, is exactly what I have been in my life.

Diedra—wanderer – alt to Deirdre (Gaelic)

Dierdre—sorrowful, wanderer

I have always been a wanderer in a world where it seems I do not belong. Moreover, because of my strikes, and other events in my life, I have been a woman often filled with sorrow. Can a sorrowful wanderer find Joy?

Joy – The world cannot give it and the world cannot take it away. There is no real joy in the world. This is only joy of the skin, joy of the flesh. There is no spiritual joy in our world. So, no, I could not find real joy in my situation if it were not for the promise of God. This book revolves so much around the Spiritual aspect because I learned that with three strikes in this world, you are truly out unless you have the Savior.

Our joy comes from God, from a spiritual place only. It comes through:

Prince of Peace

King of Kings

Shelter in a Time of Storm

God gives us peace when our world is full of turmoil. God is our King when we feel like nothing but a servant to this world. In addition, when the battles, both spiritual and physical, rage all around us, God is our Shelter from that storm.

God says to us, when we trust in Him through hard times, "Since you have kept my commandments and waited patiently, there are blessings for the keepers." You reap rewards in this life and in the next. That is what UA is. It is that time of commitment to God that no matter how bad things might be all around us, we are staying faithful because we trust in Him. We trust that our lives will be changed no matter what our situation. We trust that He will raise us up.

God will rescue you from Tribulation. He promises to us, "Since you have kept my word, I'm going to rescue you from the worst that it could be." This is another reason we must stay true to God when we are not ready or wanting Him around. It is always best for us to maintain a faithful relationship with God in the good and in the bad. It is not enough to stick true to God in the good times. We must stay with him in the bad. We must stay with God and be true at all times, even in the best and worst of times. We must always be ready for those blessings for they might come when we are not ready.

Madeline and I used to talk about the timing of our births. If I had been born in the period of slavery, they would have killed me because I was defective. Madeline said if she were born at another time prior to her actual birth, she would have never made it through childhood. At the age of two, she had convulsions and severe asthma. God's timing for us is perfect. He wanted me to live and thus I was born now, today, to learn the UA courses and pass them on to you.

My friend Madeline and I did not have to meet. We could have crossed paths without noticing. We could have never bonded or continued that first conversation. We could have walked separate paths, unwilling to accept the blessing God had in store for each of us at the time we met. However, because of our faith, tested though it was, God put us together right when we needed it. You know one reason my walk with God is so exciting? Because I do not know who I will meet tomorrow. I do not know who God will put in my life from day to day.

One day I might meet someone to lift me up. The next, I might meet the person God needs me to lift. How exciting to know every morning God is going to do something in my life? You have that same promise.

Early Christians were once warned of a time they would face great Roman persecution. And in time, that time came. They were killed, treated as second-class citizens, treated without rights, and God has rewarded their faith with the faith of this country. The early Christians had an immediate reference for these warnings.

Immediate reference—To the Roman persecution which was going to inflicted on the church. Did you know Paul was one of the worst persecutors of Christians? He was known as a ruthless killer of Christians. Until God grabbed hold of him and turned him into the best missionary of all time. Never give up on those around you.

Today we are given an even greater reference. It is possible we are just around the corner from the ultimate reference. It is also one that will come when we least expect it. It is the one you better be ready for. God says this Ultimate Reference will come when we least expect it.

Ultimate Reference—the Great Tribulation. The church will be raptured and the fury of the devil will be unleashed. We'll experience a time of great trial, perhaps now, and then we'll all be called away from this Earth and these trials, to be taken up into Heaven with God. Then the Earth will be turned over to Satan, and God's people will be saved.

No matter how bad things are, the Lord is going to keep you from the worst they could be. This is going to be the worst time our world has ever known just prior to the best time we have ever known. Before God gives our world freedom from all sin, all pain, and yes friends, all adversity...there will be a great tribulation. Should we have to go through that tribulation, commit with me to stay true to God. No matter what we face, we must remain true to His word and trust in His promises.

Praise Him for the things that you know He has kept you from.

Praise Him for the things that you do not know He has kept you from.

He has kept me from death. He did not have to, but kept me free and safe when I was dropped on my head. From that day forward, God had His hand on me. There was no question once I learned of God's goodness that He had always been there. In hindsight, it is often easier to see than when you are looking into the future. However, if you can look back knowing God was there, you should be able to trust that He will be there for your every tomorrow.

I am glad to know that God knows how much you can handle. Trust Him in that. I do not know why the Lord puts certain tribulations on some people that he does not put on everybody. Nobody can answer why hundreds of thousands of people were killed in the great tsunami. However, God is with those survivors, and Christians around the world are pouring out their love and prayers on the suffering. We do not know why, but we know we are called to help in the time of need.

When the Lord puts you through certain tribulations that is because He deems you strong enough to handle it. Take your tribulations with the heart they are meant, to test and take on your core strength. Demonstrate to those around you, humbly, that you can rise above the worst. Let them lend a hand, and believe God sent them your way.

God is not going to give you more than you can handle, but He will give you all you can handle.

There are two things you need to remember for this chapter.

1) That in the UA you can pass with honors.

Trust in God for those times where you feel you are being tested.

2) Receive a bonus—Pass with honors.

The coming of the Lord may be good or bad news. Contingent, of course, upon your condition. The coming of Christ is a warning from those who have not received him, but assurance for that who have accepted Him. God wants all generations to live with the mindset that He is coming back soon. When He comes, the implication is that the "keepers" are going to wear a crown. The NT talks about the different levels of faithfulness to be fit to wear a crown. The crown is not salvation. Salvation has already been bought with the crucifixion so it is free. Depending on your level of faithfulness determines whether you get the bonus.

Since my life is predestined, the Lord already knows if I am going to pass, pass with honors, or fail, and have to retake the coarse road. When you pass with honors, you will receive a bonus—a crown. A crown signifies accomplishments when you excelled beyond the targeted mark. There awaits a crown with my name on it.

Crowns represent faithfulness even after admission to Heaven. Crowns you work for, Salvation you believe for. We are taught that salvation does not come by work. We are not saved by our works, but by our faith. However, our works earn us a crown. We earn a mansion in Heaven based on our works. After all, faith without works is dead. So while you might still be saved by your faith, you might be dead spiritually without works.

Keep the word of God, follow his lead, and believe that he is the Pillar of your life.

Reinforced as a Pillar—Pillar means stability to those of you who have been faithful and kept my word.

God keeps those who keep His word. God will rapture those, in the final days, who keep His word. He keeps those that praise Him in good times and in bad times.

Paul looks forward to the resurrection and states that the Lord will award me and other believers. Through our good works, Paul says we can earn the Crown of Righteousness. In Revelations, believers under persecution are told to be faithful even to death, and I will give you a Crown of Life. Works and faith, faith even in times of promised persecution, earn us the bonuses in Heaven. They are promised to us when we take life in God's eyes, and not in our own limited view.

Our greatest glory is not in never failing, but in rising up every time we fail.

- Ralph Waldo Emerson

What Will They Say?

Time for another list of questions. These are not easy to answer either, but they are part of the UA curriculum. Nobody likes to think about death. However, death is a consequence of the gift of life. Someday we will each die. Take a few minutes and think about these questions based on where you life is at the moment. For the first question, do not answer based on what you "hope," but based on today, where your life is right now.

What will they say about you when they pay tribute at your funeral?

What would you like for them to say? What legacy do you want to leave?

What can you do to get close to this legacy?

Enoch walked with God. I came close to death several times and God pulled me through. What events happened in your life to make you have a closer walk with God?

Have you reached a point in your work for God where you can say, "Let my works speak for me."?

Do you have a record of helping others as God has lifted you?

Do not forget, I am not promoting salvation by works. This is not a book about receiving eternal life, necessarily. However, in order to lift you out of your pit of despair, or to overcome your three strikes, it is vital that you do good works for others. Because while works do not save us, faith without works is dead.

So, again, of what will your eulogy consist? Make a list of what you would like to be remembered for.

How close are you to completing that list?

What can you do in the next months and years to leave the legacy you want?

You must express a dependency and an appreciation of all that God gives us. People rarely give credit to those around them who help them in life. It is important to remember to give those who have helped you credit where it is due. While it takes effort for us to remember to give that credit, how much more difficult is it to remember to give God some credit? Moreover, how much more spine does it take to look at our friends and say, "God did this for me?" We call it testifying. In Wal-Mart, can you stand and testify? It is important to give testimony at church. However, it is also important to spread that appreciation so that on your final day, they can say at your funeral, "God was good, and we know it because we were constantly told of His good works."

Testimony- Publicly giving God praise for a specific blessing.

I developed a progressive walk with God. As an adult, I often went against the grain of popular opinion. People often thought they knew more about my situation than I did. Have you ever had someone tell you exactly what you should do in this or that situation? Moreover, they do not have any idea what you are going through? I had all kinds of advice from well-wishers who did not know what my situation was, or what was best for me to do.

We do that as people because we all have areas of expertise. However, we forget to consider the feelings and motivation of those around us. We forget to put ourselves in others' shoes.

People (doctors, some family) confused my determination with stubbornness. But I was always on top of it. I almost always trusted that God was in control, and that I must only obey. The three strikes are character builders. People looking at me may see weakness, but I see my problems (or my strikes) as 500lb. weights that I can lift over my head. Jesus met me where I was.

I did not want to let others tell me what was what. I did not want what others' thought to be the reality. My words must speak for me. I was and I am determined to be all that God wants me to be, not what those around me want me to become.

We all desire to be thought of highly. We all want people to say nice things about us. However, while we work, sometimes we have to follow our hearts and do well for others without the recognition. Oftentimes, it is not visible to those around us what we have done to improve the lives around us. However, in time we get that recognition. We might be gone, they might not talk about it until we have left a legacy, but that legacy will lift others. Do not look for recognition now. Look to walk with God.

Perhaps your eulogy dream should be that person after person goes forward to testify that you have helped them when nobody else would. How exciting would it be to sit with God watching your own funeral and hearing all these people were truly helped by your works? It is not about getting rewards here, it is about helping others live more comfortable lives. Then, we get our crown in Heaven. Moreover, we get the bonus of feeling like we have done our best for fellow humans. Regardless of their color, age, strikes, or profession. We are all children of God, and this should never be forgotten.

There are blessings in walking with God:

1) Protection—does not matter what you are going through. It is who is going through it with you. God will protect you because He knows you are being faithful. Even when it is not obvious, God is right there.

2) Direction—Guide When you think you are lost, God gives you direction. When you simply do not know which way to turn, turn anyway and trust that God is right there.

3) Instruction—Insight. The Holy Spirit can provide instruction. What others might interpret as my stubbornness is mostly my trusting in God's instruction. Whether it is instruction through scripture or instruction through meditation and prayer, I always followed God's instruction and insight. It has never failed me.

4) Relationship—God walks with us We all have nice relationships with family members or friends. However, a relationship with God is what keeps us moving forward without fear.

In this world of rewards, there are three heavens.

1) The created universe beyond Earth.

Science tells us there are more galaxies and planets within our Universe than we can imagine. It teaches us there may be more Universes than we can imagine. God created an incredible system that our most intelligent scientists may never be able to crack.

2) The spiritual home of God. The realm of God.

God says through Isaiah the heavens are higher than the Earth, so are my ways higher than your ways and my thoughts are higher than your thoughts. The spiritual home of God is both Heaven, and within us. Because God is made up of a Holy Trinity, the Holy Spirit (made of God) lives within us. Therefore, we have a Heaven within, and a Heaven above.

3) The Heavens and Earth

The total material world is often linked to the statements of God's cosmic purpose.

It is not because things are difficult that we do not dare, it is because we do not dare that they are difficult. - Seneca

University of Adversity Check-Up

Learned or instilled traits that will help you excel at the University of Adversity.

1) Have an exceptional purpose

2) Are willing to step out in faith

3) Possess an attitude of belonging

4) Are committed to life-long learning

5) Strive for health in all aspects of their lives—Mind, Body, & Soul

Chapter Ten
From Hopelessness to Wholeness

In our final chapters, we're going to examine how by now you should be filled with hope that no matter what strikes you brought to this book, you can walk away whole. The University of Adversity coursework is coming to a close as far as practical learning is concerned. You are only at the start, though. In fact, you could read back through this book annually, or twice a year, and find that you are still learning. You will find that you still have far to go, as we all do. There can never be too many reminders of where we should be with God.

Jesus never leaves a person in the same condition as He found them. God is a God of change. No matter your condition when you enter UA, you will not leave the same. If you take all the advice in this book and try to find who God meant for you to become, you cannot leave the same. It is a never-ending challenge, of course, but it is a time to embrace all that God has in store for you. Once I found the secrets of UA, I turned from a woman with three strikes and a bleak future into someone able to put her thoughts on paper and challenged countless numbers to change their lives.

When you started reading this book, you were the old you. No matter whether you have answered the questions or not, you have still changed in some way. If you answered the questions honestly, and read the material with an open mind, you have changed a lot. You have allowed God to touch you, if only a bit. God does not leave a person the same. My prayer is that you have changed at least a little.

One important idea you must get before you can say you've passed this phase of UA is the idea that hopelessness is not necessary for life, even when you're surrounded by what seems to be nothing but hopelessness. You cannot live that way. You should not.

Helplessness stunts dreams and causes you to settle for mediocrity.

When you feel helpless, you will feel you cannot reach those inner dreams. You will settle for mediocrity. However, you cannot. You must not. God wants you to overcome the helplessness you feel by realizing you have great worth. In your worth, you will find your individuality. In your individuality, you will find God. With this combination, you will reach your dreams, and you cannot settle for mediocrity. When we sit around hoping for more out of life, we should be aware at that moment that we are enmeshed in mediocrity. Rise above that and realize you are not helpless.

Physical Hopelessness—Sustained affliction. Makes time, and the future, seem endless and hopeless.

Sustained affliction and physical hopelessness will keep you out of your game. You will not get the blessing you deserve, that is waiting for you, if you give in to the hopelessness of physical adversity. You have reached down deeper than that to find who you are. In a hopeless situation, you will sit and watch time pass you by. You will not be able to live your life in a state of hopelessness. UA will help lift you out of that. By reading this book, you should have already come to the realization that in God, you can be healed spiritually. You can use your physical affliction for good. You can reach to those around you; you can live your dreams.

Psychological Hopelessness—When doctors cannot cure you.

You will be kept down and out of the game of life in a psychological way if you are told there is no hope for you. I was told time and again, there was no hope for me. If I had believed this and held tight, there would be no way I would be alive today. Even if I were alive, I would in no way be writing a book or trusting in God. I could not possibly have the assurance in myself if I had bought into what doctors said and what they were telling me. Overcome this by studying in this class through, UA and trust in God.

Social Hopelessness—Outcast from society.

You cannot worry about fitting in until you feel certain of yourself. You must be strong as an individual or you will never fit into society. It is only once you feel that you are truthfully yourself that you will be able to show society who you really are. Even if you live different, act different, look different, society will still respects people who respect themselves. You will not be an outcast once you show society you do not belong in the outcast category. It is possible to fit in even when you never have simply by accepting who you are.

Economic Hopelessness— being unable to financially sustain a minimum standard of living.

When you are disabled and have to be deemed impoverished to get adequate government assistance. No incentive. They set you up to fail. There is no incentive to go out, get a job, and lift yourself out of poverty while you are being given government assistance. Assistance is necessary when you have no choice, but there is no incentive to better yourself. As a result, you fail and the government has the control over your limited choices. You feel economic hopelessness. However, God will lift you out of that hopelessness. You will land on your own two feet because your incentive is internal. You want to better yourself because you have discovered your individualism. You cannot fail your individual self. It is an internal incentive.

New Beginning

The UA gives yourself a New Beginning. You get a new lease on life. Everything will come together once you feel you have a grasp on what God wants for you. You become an individual. Through the UA, you can become everything you are meant to become. It is a good way to get yourself in the right place for when those blessings come.

God and the UA give you hope. In one or more areas of life right now, you might feel hopeless. You can be lifted from this hope by your choices, your actions, and your attitude. You will be given hope. Once you start looking forward to your future, whether financial or social, you will be delivered from your strikes.

Your three strikes will go away, and you will be lifted above them to a new height.

Deliverance starts:

1) When you hear the right thing

This book, the University of Adversity coursework, is a means of hearing the right news at the right time. Once you hear the good news that hope is alive, you begin to gain deliverance.

2) In the right place

You are in the right place. Put your practice to work, think over the questions and answers above and you will find other hopeless people all around. Those folks are waiting for you to help lift them up.

3) Have the right faith

Jesus has a way of honoring our faith even if it is not as mature as it supposed to be. You will gain trust and love for God through UA. It might not be a mature faith, a faith that can move mountains. However, sometimes is the new faith that is as pure as new fallen snow. God loves that purity of thought. He will reward it the moment you turn it over to Him.

Jesus recognizes the value of a person. You cannot hide from your potential. You can deny it, you can forget about it, you can pretend there is nothing in your value, but Jesus knows your value. Do not try to stay away from it. Why would you? If you find yourself in a pit of despair, and if you have moments of hopelessness in your life, what is the use in denying what God wants you to become. Give into Him, and lift yourself into deliverance. Become whole.

We live scattered lives in a world that moves fast. Our families are dysfunctional, our bank accounts are small, and our dreams are high. We want wholeness, but how do we know when we are there? How did I know when my life was all I wanted it to be?

What does wholeness look like?

1) New Personhood.

When Jesus is done with, you are a new person. People will label you by your condition. Nevertheless, when you are God's person, and labeled God's person, you are given a new person. You are given a new Peace. That new Peace is wholeness, and you will feel it. You will know that you are changed.

2) Deliverance from the place you find your hopelessness.

What if you have problems with dandelions in your yard? You can mow them over and they will go away for a few days. However, that is not enough. You have to get to the root. Find out what the ROOT CAUSE is. Once you pull up the root, once you dig inside yourself and find out what's going on within, God will lift you from your hopelessness. Then, and only once you reach the root, can you find true wholeness.

Do not let this opportunity pass you by. You have this day, this moment, to become whole. Grab your problems by the root, jerk them free, and become one with God. Jesus specializes in hopeless cases.

Never, never, never give up.
- Winston Churchill

Black and (but) Beautiful

Poems—Allegory

But- Conjunction Adversative Conjunction

The world says, "Hey she's black, but she's beautiful." That word "but" joins two concepts that are not consistent with one another. The word 'but' brings in a negative connotation. We are still living in a world where somebody might say that. However, here is what I have to say.

I am black, and I am beautiful. Period. There is no separation between the two words. Beyond even this issue there are negative connotations to the word black. Think about all the ways we use the word black in a negative way. There is an inconsistency between two sides.

Society's negative connotation for BLACK.

Blacklisted- Public person shunned for speaking up on a controversial topic.

Black Sheep- Family member who is not living up to expectations.

Black Monday- When the stock market crashed.

Dark Horse- A public figure who is expected to lose an election and then suddenly starts to emerge.

Whose definition do we use to define beauty? Many times beauty is something defined by media, or by the cover of magazines. It is not just left to those people to tell us, though.

We have to agree. We have to fall in line and agree that those are the beautiful people and that the rest of us are the average or below average.

Even more, sometimes in our own community we do not define blackness with beauty. We look all over the rest of society to find beauty, and we miss so much more of it right within our own community. We are looking for the wrong things. We need to look at one another in the same way God looks at us. I do not believe God sees colors. I do not believe our Souls have color, and God sees us all the same. It is time we see everyone the same.

We must get rid of the 'black but beautiful' mentality and move into a mentality where beautiful can be more within, and color has nothing to do with it.

In addition, "and" is a connective conjunction which means what is on either side of the conjunction naturally goes together.

I am black and beautiful.

I am beautiful.

God made me—sense of self-worth.

Growing up in the city, you only know your own world. I was sheltered within my own community. I thought black meant poor; it meant a second or third class citizen. Unless you were an actor or an athlete, you did not get 'out' of your circumstances. When I left home at 19, I was shocked to see more prominent, affluent African Americans. I did not realize you could achieve your dreams regardless of where you lived or who you were.

Tracey would not like to come alone to my house because I lived in the city. She said her mother told her that someone could steal your car. I told her that your car could be stolen even in the suburbs where she lived. Crime happens anywhere. Our friendship shortly ended. I was not going to be ashamed of where I live or who I am.

When you close your mind to options and the potential within yourself, or others, you keep yourself bound. You are like a rubber band wrapped around your wheelchair, you are pressing with all your might and making little strides. You cannot move forward because you are trapped in your own world, a world separate from reality. Whether you are black or white, if you close your eyes to the world and possibilities around you, you stop yourself in your tracks.

You must press on. You must press outside your boundaries. You must open your eyes to those around you, to the potential within yourself, and open you are heard to God.

Press through racial intolerance.

Press through the physical, psychological, emotional and spiritual pain of disability.

Press through the stereotypes.

Words and Effect

Along with the idea that the color 'black' is used in negative connotations worldwide, and therefore helps to add a strike to our condition, there is also the word effect. Words within our language, within the black culture, are often times construed as uneducated language. It is a tool used against us when we try to break through that glass ceiling.

Black Slang – once considered 'Ebonics' and banned in certain schools. Now, it is being realized as a cultural language no different from Appalachian 'slang' or upper New England 'slang.'

One popular word that is used in our everyday language is 'Word.' As in a greeting to a friend, "Word," or to confirm enthusiasm for something one might say, "Word up!" Now you see this usage in movies, on the street, even in white circles. It has become part of the language, and only because we refused to admit what society expected of us is right. Our culture is right, it is correct, and we will not be changed. The world approached us with an open mind, and we prevail.

Word - Usually used as a means of conveying agreement. It is the modern version of "right on." This expression was mainly used in the early '90s.

Word, The

n. Any type of slang, info, or gossip.

Acknowledgement, approval, indication of enthusiasm.

"Dude, count me in, word up!"

P.O.N.S – Press On Nubian Scholar/Latin –Bridge

Since this bridge is made from divine construction, then what are you pressing? You are pressing from all the trouble that is hitting you while you are trying to cross the bridge.

In our present time, there is much emphasis put on our access points. How to guard them from the physical threat of terrorists attacks. We must also protect our personal 'access points.' Where we are vulnerable, we need to examine and figure out ways to protect those areas of ourselves. Are you vulnerable in the area of drinking? You need to protect that with all your might. Perhaps you are vulnerable to criticism of your 'strikes.' You need to figure out how to accept those strikes and those areas cease to be access points of vulnerability.

From One Sister to Another

When Bessie Delaney was young, she asked her parents why did white people hate us so much? Her mother replied, "Because they think we don't have souls." Earlier in the book I have discussed the real discrimination in the mind of society, especially the South, as late as the 1960's. In some places, even today. People can actually look at an African-American and believe we are without souls or that we are without worth as humans or as people. Our love of family is never considered.

Our love of neighbor and of country is never considered. We have come a long way, true. However, in many places we have a long way to go. It starts with us. It starts with our believing God is on our side, and that we are worthy.

Naomi and her two daughters-in-law, Orpah and Ruth, did not contemplate suicide when their husbands died. They believed in life and forged ahead, even when their very lives were changed.

Singer Phyllis Hyman committed suicide because "*Love Life*" was not what she thought it should be. Her values and self-importance were not in the right perspective. She allowed her access points to remain wide-open, and when the unimportant things failed, she thought she was a failure. Society beat her down, and she allowed it.

We cannot allow it. We have to build character strong enough to stand against all oppression. Whether societal or personal, we cannot allow ourselves to be open to attack.

Strength in Character—if she only knew Jesus. If she only felt intoxicated with his love, and not with her own selfish weaknesses. She could have survived. How many people do you know that kill themselves out of desperation? Isn't gang fighting just another form of suicide? Weakness and fighting over unimportant things? It is all about the lack of character, and the lack of Jesus in our lives.

Be who you are. There is no challenge not to be who I am. I am automatically going to be me in spite of circumstances. There is a difference between character and reputation.

Some people can act out of character and care more about reputation. Positive behavior represents the best quality of who you are. Own up to who you are despite temptation. Even when you leave church you should act like a Christian. Whoever you are, be a positive example even more so in tough times.

Who you are. The Lord wants to take control of who you are. He does not parcel certain pieces leaving the rest to us. God puts us here for a reason and in spite of obstacles; He will get you to where you need to be.

Prerequisite to directing is following. In order for God to show us the way, we must follow. God wants to show us the way, but do we really want to follow? Ask yourself.

Are you ready to follow?

The measure of a man is the way he bears up under misfortune.
- Plutarch

Glass Ceiling

Society will elevate you to a certain level. No matter what you do in life, society will put you someplace based on stereotypes. Once you hit a certain level, and can rise no more, we call that the glass ceiling. You have reached your stopping point in the eye of society once you become whatever it is your stereotype is expected to achieve. A handicapped African-American woman is not expected to go very far. If I had paid attention to society's glass ceiling, I would not have finished school. I might not have attended college at all. I would not believe in myself and my potential. However, I ignored the glass ceiling. Even more, I raised the glass ceiling. I redefined it.

The glass ceiling is relevant to all three strikes. Black people have inherited the strength to persevere. Now we must make our ancestors proud. Not through violence, but by working hard to break through the glass ceiling again. We can, little by little, redefine that glass ceiling. I believe without question there are pockets of society rooting for us, ready to give us the chance. God has put good people all over the country that believe all people, regardless of race or handicap, can achieve great things. We must give positive references to black single parent families. Society focuses the negative, and so do we at times. However, we can change that.

Individuals can excel when there are cracks in the ceiling. The work of the Glass Ceiling Commission cannot be separated from the ongoing public discourse of Affirmative Action, equal opportunity, and diversity. Why does it take legislation for protected classes to be permitted to evoke their rights or have their rights protected?

Stereotypes, racism, sexism live side-by-side with underachievement, worthlessness, and poverty. They feed off one another to perpetuate a cycle of unfulfilled aspirations among women and people of color. The Civil Rights Acts of 1964, expanded in 1991 to include two forms of sexual harassment prohibited by title VII. We have the protection we need. Now we need the inner belief to rise to our potential. No matter your strikes, it is time. It is time to rise above.

When you have been called by God to have a relationship, or to do things for God sometimes it may feel uncomfortable. God's love goes beyond all knowledge. God has set provisions and He is waiting for me to take hold of it. My steps have been ordered. I have to make choices for my life. If I had waited for others to make those decisions, I would be nowhere. I made steps, and I must continue to take those steps.

God has sovereign reign over human error. Do not be afraid to take chances and risk failure. A nurse once dropped me on my head as a baby. I was changed, but God worked through that human error. Not even an overdose is beyond God's healing. We must believe in order to whole. We must trust in order to get out of hopelessness.

You can break through whatever glass ceiling is just above you.

Chapter Eleven
Change Your World

What kind of person does God use?

If you have not figured it out by now, God uses the willing. We talked about Biblical examples; we have talked about real life examples. I am an example. God did not have to use me, but He wanted to. First, He gave me life, then he saved my life, then He saved my eternal soul. For all this, isn't it the least I can do to show Him gratitude?

Saving me was such an amazing act. In showing gratitude, the next step is to let God use me.

Not everyone can be used in the same capacity. Just like the Body, the people of God each play a different role. Some are the hands, some are the eyes, and some are the mouth. Ask God to give direction, and when you are ready to follow, He will show you your role. With that role, you move forward in faith. You touch those around you, and one by one, you change your world.

If everyone changes their world then eventually it will change The World.

The Lord told Gideon he wanted him to save his people from bondage. Gideon told the Lord that he was the least of the least. God used Gideon because of his humility. Do not forget that before God we are all just servants. More important than all the gold in the world is the humility that God seeks in us which allows us to be used by him.

Delayed Destiny

Moses found himself in a place where he was not supposed to be. He found himself in Midian. He was either supposed to be in Egypt with his people or liberating his people from bondage. Moses thought he was the only one that knew he killed an Egyptian, but he was not. He tried to conceal the killing. His disobedience forced him to relocate. We can set ourselves back by trying to conceal things from God.

Take a moment and answer these final questions in your journey through the University of Adversity.

What are you concealing from God that you need to tell Him? First, write it. We will talk to Him after we have completed this list.

Are there things in your life you need to give up, right now? Things keeping you from God. List them.

Have you accepted God into your life and asked Him to be your Guide?

Write three things you would really like this year. It can even be material, but check your motives before listing them. Do not let your selfishness get in the way of this exercise.

Can you commit to reading this book at least once a year and answering all the questions on an annual basis?

Are you committed to the task set forth by the University of Adversity?

Are you ready to change your world? Do you feel worthy, willing, and able?

Do you have any strikes you have not accepted as part of your person? Have we, together, overcome our strikes?

Isaiah said, "Our sins like the wind drive us away." Moses encountered God in a burning bush, and realized that it was not a bush on fire. It is not a burning bush, it's a flame concealed by a bush. Whatever the flame represents cannot be seen in its nakedness. The unnatural presence of God incarnates itself in nature. God could not, and cannot, reveal Himself in His true form. So he came to Moses in a flame, and He came to us in a different form. And the word became flesh.

God came to us in the form of Christ Jesus, allowing us to take our lives under our control. You see, the evil has already been defeated in the grand scheme of things. Now, it is up to us to break free of those shackles keeping us down and allowing God to work through us as He has worked through people for centuries. He has always used normal people to make waves, people who once thought they had 'strikes' against them.

A) Look at the glory of His appearance.

B) Look at the goal of His appearance. The goal of God was to get the attention of Moses. *The intention was to get the attention of Moses.* God uses unusual phenomenon to get your attention. Do not always wonder why things happen – it just could be to get your attention.

C) Look at the grace of His appearance. Some of the grace is implied in the text. Most people would have given up on Moses. There was nothing inherently holy about the ground itself. As Moses gets close to the bush, the Lord says, "Stop, you're approaching holy ground." What makes the ground holy is it serve the purpose of God and embodied the presence of God.

D) Look at the assignment of Moses. God was sending him back to Egypt where he had killed. God has wisdom over who he uses. Moses' disobedience may delay his destiny, but it will not destroy it.

There is a bridge between your disobedience and destiny. This bridge is called GRACE. Remember that grace is a gift, not something you earn. Grace is a safety net upon which you can fall, and God is there to catch you.

The time to repair the roof is when the sun is shining.
- John F. Kennedy

A Faith You Can Sleep With

How terrible false advertising is when you have one set of expectations and you experience a different reality. In our religious landscape, there is a lot of false advertising. Televangelists promise you health, wealth, success, prosperity, and all of these are fine if you are focused on temporal gain. God never promised these things. They do not mention God, Jesus, salvation, sanctification, salvation. If you have your mind on larger things, then you need *A Faith You Can Sleep With.*

This faith can wake you, raise you when you fall, then you need a greater religious mindset. Certain friends and certain things are supposed to help you but are retarding your progress.

How Can Jesus sleep on a sinking ship? The Bible tells of a story where Jesus slept through a storm so severe, grown men wept for their lives. Jesus never doubted their safety. He slept sound in the Grace, in the safety net, of God.

Rather than doubt his compassion, emulate His composure. Jesus knows something we need to learn.

1) There are natural occurrences that are bound to happen in certain situations. Storms will rock the boat.

2) Storms are temporary. Even when God made it rain it had a beginning and an end. Sometimes we confuse severity with duration. We think because it is hard it is eternal.

Anticipatory joy. Joy on credit. The Lord will make a way somehow.

3) Jesus knows that God always has the last word. Sickness may have the first word. Sorrow may have the second word. Oppression may have the third word, but God has the last word. Sometimes that is all you have is the word of God. God gave me a word: this book.

All labor that uplifts humanity has dignity and importance and should be undertaken with painstaking excellence. - Dr. Martin Luther King Jr.

Graduation from the University of Adversity

So, here we are. Our last few moments together. At the beginning of the book I wrote, "Not just creating change or making change but *activating* change." The U of A is about activating change first in your life, and then in your world. You come to those changes first by accepting you are weak, by taking those weaknesses you consider strikes against you and rising above them. You have to remember not to blame others for your problems, but rather to take responsibility for change upon yourself.

Jeremiah accused God of allowing the guilty to prosper. However, sustained adversity will make all of us question the

Word of God. Sustained for me were affliction, hardship, and tribulation. I stopped blaming others for my issues, and began to take on the responsibility of them myself.

God said, "What you are going through is designed to strengthen you." I began a walk in the University of Adversity without knowing I was enrolled. The outcome of the course was a bowed head and a bended knee.

If small things get you down what are you going to do when BIG things come?

When you get closer to God, adversity is going to come. He wants you to trust Him.

Remember our acronym HOPE?

HOPE- *Harnessing Optimism through Personal Experience*

God moves us from one level of maturity to another. Once we embrace our failings and failures, we reach a new level of maturity. We need to get beyond blaming others for our problems. Our lives can be changed by our daily decisions, and our small changes, day after day, add up to large changes.

Adversity will make you strong or bitter. It is up to you which end you come out on. Decide whether you will allow your adversity to take you down. You can close this book and remain bitter. You can close this book and decide today, right now, that you are going to take responsibility for your life and your community this very day. It's attitude, and it is up to you.

There should be no such thing as a bitter Christian. You might know people who claim to be walking with God and yet are still bitter. I challenge you to ask that person how it is that God wants them to live a life of bitterness. If they cannot answer, assume they do not know God as well as they profess. Be an example. Rise up against your adversity, and show the world that, through God, we do not have time to be bitter. Whatever comes our way, pray to God to make it a lesson.

God sends every Christian something he cannot handle. He does this to keep us praying, humble, and walking in His way.

If following God got you into trouble, following God will get you out of trouble. How often does walking with God lead us into situations we would not have gotten into otherwise? If we get into trouble of some sort because of God, expect that He will pull you back out. Remember how we all end up in a pit at times in our life? We have to depend upon ourselves for escape, and we have to learn to rely on others to get us out. Sometimes we are put in pits to learn to trust others to get out. It is always about lessons learned, and about lessons, we can share with others.

The good news about the University of Adversity is that you cannot get a C+. It is a Pass/Fail Curriculum

If you pass, you pass with Honors.

If you fail, you simply try again. You take the course over. You should face each of these questions and issues with more seriousness. Moreover, you need to come to God with all your heart. If you come to God with your heart, if you face your adversity, if you take responsibility for your own life and mistakes, and you then pass it on, then you pass.

Then what?

Continuing Education—work for a crown. Become a professional student enrolled in the University of Adversity.

When I was a pre-teen, I asked my cousin Larry, who is nine years older than me, "Is there such a thing as a professional student?" He said, "No." He did not know about the University of Adversity.

Graduation just means you move onto another adversity. Graduation makes you stronger for the next adversity.

Because you are stronger, the next adversity may be tougher. In this world, the odds are never against us. Not in God-terms. But it might seem that they are. In fact, the idea of three strikes is that 'you're out.' Once you are out, you are supposed to not be able to play the game anymore. Therefore, these three strikes make us think we are completely out of the game. At least that the odds are so stacked against us we are out of luck. We cannot let our internal fears keep us down. We cannot let how the world perceives us influence how we perceive ourselves.

Your adversity is unique, because you are unique. No matter what your strikes, they are unique to you. How you handle those strikes will be unique to you as well. It is important to remember you are not alone, and that you are not just a clone in a crowd either. You are a unique individual in a society that is truly a melting pot. It might seem at times a certain group of thinkers are running the show. It is not so. The show is run by those that move, and the University of Adversity challenges you to get up and move.

Adapt, improvise, and overcome, not just a good motto for marines. You must adapt to the changes that come your way. Some of those changes might be negative, others are positive. Regardless, you must adapt to those changes and improvise how you deal with change. Think fast on your feet. Believe that you can do this and you will find when you least expect it that you will overcome everything tossed in your path. Financial, health, relationships…no matter the bump in the road, you can turn it to your advantage with planning, action, and determination.

Never be too proud to ask the Lord for help. In fact, get in the habit of thanking Him for the good and for the bad. Ask Him when you have questions. Let Him know when you have doubts. It is okay to wrestle with God as long as your heart is with Him.

The Lord never gives more then you can handle. You might be in the process of being tested. You might be pushed to a limit you do not think you can live with. However, He will not give you more than you can handle. Thank Him when He shows you just how strong you truly are. Thank Him for lifting you out of where you were, and into a new world. In this world of UA, you can take anything thrown at you and come through it with a deeper faith, a stronger will, and making an impact on your world.

As we mentioned earlier, there are learned or instilled traits that will help you excel at the University. After you finish this book, after you are finished, you should run a checklist to make sure you have followed each of these traits. They are a demonstration to the world. Once you begin to demonstrate the traits below, you will be well on your way to success within the UA. Remember, the UA never actually ends. It is a lifelong learning process. So if you cannot pick up all the traits below quickly, be patient. Pray for them, and God will make you aware of them in time.

Discipline
Faith
Love
Hope
Compassion
Discretion

The ways and means that we use to overcome our adversity is what molds our character. We are only a result of our choices. Sometimes life throws things at us for which we are not prepared. It is a guarantee. Nevertheless, you can make the choice to overcome every single curve ball. Hey, if the Boston Red Sox can win a World Series, you can easily, without question, take control of your life. This is your moment. Today is your day.

When you close this book, remember the slogan of a simple shoe commercial, Nike. Just Do It. It is simple, it is a pat answer, but you must. Where would I be if I had not stood and took my life into my own hands? What would have become of me? I shudder to think. It is this reason I come to you, begging you to take back your life.

For decades, African-Americans have overcome everything put in their way. In a matter of a couple of generations we've come from being seen as sub-human to having athletic stars, powerful members of Hollywood, powerful personages in politics, even two appointed officials third in line to the President. It is amazing. You see, we can do anything we want when we walk with God. We must keep up the momentum regardless of our skin color. We are moving toward a better day. We want no more war, but peace. We want financial freedom, not bondage to creditors. We want leadership positions, not subservient roles. We want a voice, not be pawns in a game bigger than us.

It starts with you, dear friend.

I have been given this message to pass on to you. Take it, apply it, learn the coursework within the University of Adversity. Most of all, once you are in control of your life, pass it on.

Change your life, change your world.

For more information on Diedra Cole, this book, or other releases by The Empty Canoe, please visit us online at:

www.emptycanoe.com

Printed in the United States
35763LVS00005B/4-24